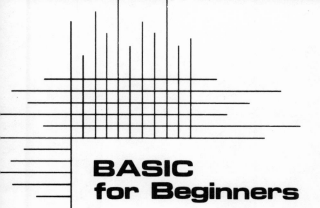

BASIC
for Beginners

BASIC

FOR BEGINNERS

by Christopher Lampton

A Computer Literacy Skills Book
FRANKLIN WATTS   1984
New York   London   Toronto   Sydney

Library of Congress Cataloging in Publication Data

Lampton, Christopher.
BASIC for beginners.

(A Computer literacy skills book)
Includes index.
Summary: Introduces the language of BASIC and
how to use it in programming a microcomputer.
Includes programming projects.
1. Basic (Computer program language)—
Juvenile literature.
2. Microcomputers—Programming—
Juvenile literature.
[1. Basic (Computer program language)
2. Microcomputers. 3. Computers.
4. Programming (computers)] I. Title.
II. Series.
QA76.73.B3L353 1984   001.64′24   83-23559
ISBN 0-531-04745-8

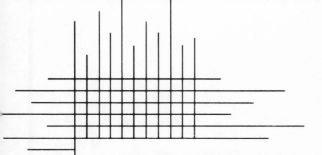

2224864

CONTENTS

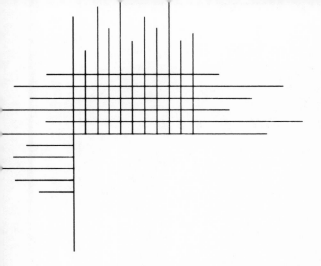

COMPUTER BOOKS BY
CHRISTOPHER LAMPTON:

COMPUTER LANGUAGES
(A Computer-Awareness First Book)

PROGRAMMING IN BASIC
(A Computer-Awareness First Book)

ADVANCED BASIC
(A Computer Literacy Skills Book)

BASIC FOR BEGINNERS
(A Computer Literacy Skills Book)

COBOL FOR BEGINNERS
(A Computer Literacy Skills Book)

FORTH FOR BEGINNERS
(A Computer Literacy Skills Book)

FORTRAN FOR BEGINNERS
(A Computer Literacy Skills Book)

PASCAL FOR BEGINNERS
(A Computer Literacy Skills Book)

PILOT FOR BEGINNERS
(A Computer Literacy Skills Book)

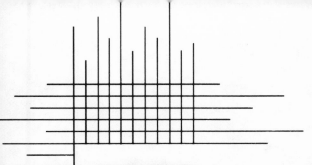

BASIC
for Beginners

1
THE MAGIC COMPUTER

In ancient times, certain words were thought to have magic powers. Today we know better, of course, but we still have magic words. The difference between modern magic words and the ancient ones is that the ancient ones didn't work. The modern ones do.

This is a book about magic. It is about the words that, when learned, will give you power over that most amazing of inventions, the computer. In it, you will find a number of magic spells, called *programs,* which will bring about miraculous transformations. If you don't believe this, just keep reading.

We live in the computer age. For better or worse, more and more aspects of our lives are becoming involved with computers.

There are those who fear that computers will soon control our lives totally. These fears are largely misplaced. Those of us who know how to control computers can have more control over our lives than ever before. Computers can only "control" those who don't understand them. That's what the idea of "computer literacy" is all about: learning how to make computers work for you.

Computers are marvelous machines. And perhaps the most marvelous thing about them is that they can be anything we want them to be, within reasonable limits. With a wave of our magic wand, we can transform a computer into

Program—A series of instructions telling a computer how to perform a task or tasks.

a video arcade game or a cash register or a word processor (which is a fancy kind of typewriter) or any of a thousand other things. To bring about this transformation, all we need is a program.

And what is a program? Simply put, it is a set of instructions that tell a computer step-by-step what we want it to do.

How do you write a program? Not in ordinary English, that's for sure. Computers, however marvelous they may be, have not yet managed a task that is literally child's play for human beings: understanding everyday language. The instructions that we give a computer in a program must be simplified and logically arranged. Fortunately, computer scientists have developed special simplified, logical languages with which we can write these instructions. These languages are called (appropriately enough) computer *programming languages.*

Because they are simpler than human languages, computer languages are more easily learned than, say, French or German (especially for those of us who failed to learn French and German early in life). In this book, we will learn a language called BASIC. The name BASIC is an abbreviation of Beginner's All-purpose Symbolic Instruction Code. BASIC was developed by professors at Dartmouth College in the mid-1960s. As its name implies, BASIC was designed for potential programmers who had little or no experience with computers. Originally, BASIC was a very simple language with a limited number of "words." It could be learned in a few days or even hours. BASIC has changed somewhat in the years since, but it is still easy to learn. More about that in a moment.

Before we begin to learn the BASIC language, however, we first must know a little about this machine that we will be "talking" with: the computer.

What is a computer?

In simplest terms, the computer is a device for manipulating information. But this is like calling an automobile a

---

Programming language—One of the languages in which a computer program must be written.

device for transporting mass. It explains what it does but loses the spirit of the thing.

When we say that a computer is a device for manipulating information, we are placing it in the same category as television sets, musical instruments, typewriters, printing presses, thermostats, and even cameras. All these things are devices for manipulating information. What sets the computer apart from the other items just listed is its versatility. With the right program, a computer can simulate the function of almost any other information-handling device, be it a musical instrument, a printing press, a typewriter, or whatever.

As we saw a moment ago, programs must be written in computer language. Contrary to what we implied, however, there is only a single language that computers understand. It is called *machine language,* and it is made up entirely of numbers. Writing computer programs made up of numbers is no simple task; fortunately, there is an alternative to writing programs in numbers.

Although computers only understand machine language, they can be programmed—that is, given a set of instructions—to understand other languages, such as BASIC. The instructions that tell the computer how to understand BASIC are written in machine language. However, once we have given the computer instructions telling it how to understand a new language, all further instructions may be written in the new language. Thus, if we are using a computer that has been programmed to understand BASIC, we may write all further programs in BASIC. Or, if we prefer to use another language, we can reprogram the computer to understand that language. These languages that a computer must be programmed to understand are called *high-level*

Machine language—The only language that a computer can understand without translation; machine-language programs consist of strings of ones and zeros.

High-level language—A computer language in which each instruction must be translated into several machine-language instructions before it can be run on a computer.

languages. BASIC is a high-level language. Other high-level languages include FORTRAN, Pascal, COBOL, LISP, Ada, and Forth.

BASIC was originally designed for use on large computers. However, the language did not become widely popular until the mid-1970s, with the arrival of microcomputers. Because most microcomputers are owned by people with little previous computer experience, a computer language that is easy to learn and use was needed. BASIC fills the bill perfectly. Furthermore, the early microcomputers were not capable of holding very large programs, and it was possible to develop very small programs for translating BASIC into machine language, whereas other languages required very large programs. (Newer, larger microcomputers have more advanced versions of BASIC.)

Over the last several years, computer programmers have developed many different versions of the BASIC language, for many different brands of microcomputers. This means that the version of BASIC that you will find on an Apple computer is not identical to the version of BASIC that you will find on a TRS-80 or an Atari. Furthermore, most modern versions of BASIC are considerably more complex than the original BASIC developed at Dartmouth in the 1960s.

Although BASIC is still an easy language to learn, an ambitious programmer is now able to use more advanced programming techniques, to go beyond the simple set of instructions that comprised the original language. Nonetheless, it remains possible to learn at least some of the basics of the BASIC language in a very short time, perhaps just a few hours.

In this book, we will assume that you have access to a microcomputer, either at home or at school, or at least will have access to one sometime in the future. In the event that you do not have a computer available, this book can still serve as an introduction to the essential concepts of computer programming. We will concentrate on the version of BASIC known as Microsoft BASIC, so-called because it was developed by the Microsoft Corporation of Bellevue, Washington. Microsoft BASIC can be found on the Apple II+ and IIe (under the name Applesoft BASIC), the TRS-80 Models I and III (as Level II and Model III BASIC), the

Radio Shack Color Computer (as Color BASIC and Extended Color BASIC), the Commodore computers (including the VIC-20, the Pet, and the Commodore 64), the IBM Personal Computer, the Mattel Aquarius, and the Spectravideo home computer. Though the versions of Microsoft BASIC used by these computers are slightly different, we will concentrate on the areas where all the versions are similar and point out differences as we encounter them. Furthermore, we will occasionally mention other versions of BASIC, when necessary giving directions for adapting programs to computers that do not run Microsoft BASIC, such as the Atari computers, the TI-99/4 and 99/4A, and the Timex Sinclair 1000 and 2068. (The Timex Sinclair 1000 is also known as the Sinclair ZX80 and ZX81.) The versions of BASIC these computers use are not terribly different from Microsoft BASIC; in fact, the differences are minor, except in the most advanced programs.

Before you can begin programming (assuming you have access to a computer), you must first know how to prepare your computer to be programmed in BASIC. Most of the computers just named are ready for programming practically from the moment that they are turned on, but in a few cases the program that allows the computer to understand BASIC must first be loaded into the computer from a magnetic disk. This is true of the TRS-80 Models I and III (systems with disk drives attached) and the IBM Personal Computer (PC). (A *disk drive* is a device that "reads" a magnetic disk the way a record player reads a record or a tape recorder reads a tape.) If no disk drive is attached to your system—on the TRS-80 Model III the disk drive will be built right into the computer—no disk will be required for programming in BASIC. On some computers, a special cartridge containing the BASIC language program must be inserted into a slot on the computer. (This is true of Atari computers, for instance, and the TI-99/4A with Extended BASIC.)

Disk drive—A device for storing information once it has been taken out of the computer. Disk drives store information on the surface of a magnetic disk.

Before you begin programming, it would be best for you to consult your computer manual, or talk to someone who has used the computer, to learn what steps you must take before you can begin programming. If all else fails, simply turn on the computer and see if it will accept BASIC programs. You can't hurt a computer simply by typing, though it's not advisable to push buttons and throw switches if you aren't sure what they do.

The next step is to take a deep breath, sit down at the computer—and turn to the next chapter.

2
WHAT THE COMPUTER CAN DO

Once you have the computer prepared for programming, the next thing to do is write a program. But let's not rush into this too quickly. First, just take a look at the computer itself. Examine its parts. Familiarize yourself with it.

If it is like most small computers, it will have a *video display*, or monitor. This will look much like an ordinary home television screen. In fact, with a great many small computers, such as the Apple and the Atari, the video display often is an ordinary home television set, attached to the computer with a short cable. The video display is the way in which the computer communicates with you. From time to time, messages will appear on this screen. And, in the course of this chapter, we will learn how to put our own messages on the display. Later, we will even discuss how to put pictures on it.

Below the television screen is the *keyboard*. On some small computers, such as the TRS-80 Models III and IV, the keyboard and the video display are combined into one unit. On most, however, the keyboard is a separate unit, attached to the video monitor, or to your home television, with a cable. If the video display is the means by which the

Video display—A device, much like a standard television set, for getting information out of the computer.

Keyboard—A device, much like the keyboard of a standard typewriter, used for putting information into a computer.

computer communicates with you, the keyboard is the means by which you communicate with the computer. There are other methods by which you can communicate with the computer, and other ways that the computer can communicate with you, but in this book we will concentrate on the video display and the keyboard, which are the most common ways of communicating with a small computer.

The keyboard looks very much like the keyboard on an ordinary typewriter, though some of the keys may be in different places or have different names. Most computers have a few keys with decidedly unusual names, such as BREAK and CTRL and CLEAR and RUN-STOP. To find out what these keys do, you can consult the user's manual, though we will discuss several of these keys in this book.

If you know how to type on a typewriter, then you know almost everything you need to know about typing on a computer keyboard. If you don't know how to type, just hunt and peck. To type a given letter into the computer, find the key with that letter written on it and press it. If there is more than one character printed on a key, one above the other, you can usually get the character on top by hitting the key while also holding down the key marked SHIFT. A few computers include several characters on each key; the user's manual will tell you how to type these characters into the computer.

On a few computers, such as the Timex Sinclair 1000 and the Atari 400, there are no real "keys," as on a typewriter. Instead, there are pressure-sensitive "membranes" where keys would normally be. These membranes cover sensitive electronic switches that are activated when the membrane is pressed. To type on these membranes, you must press firmly against them as though they actually were typewriter keys. If you are a touch typist, however, you may find the membranes frustratingly slow to respond; you'll have to restrain your enthusiasm and type more slowly. This is one case where hunt-and-peck typists may actually be at an advantage.

It should also be noted that the Timex Sinclair computers accept typed programs from the keyboard in a decidedly peculiar fashion. Most of the information in this book on how to use a computer keyboard will not apply to the Sinclair, though the programs themselves will run properly on the computer, with the modifications noted in the text. To find out how to type programs on the Sinclair, consult your manual.

After turning on your computer, you should see a *prompt*. What is a prompt? A prompt is a symbol that indicates that the computer is waiting for you to start typing. On many computers the prompt will be a greater-than sign (">"). It may be preceded by the word READY, like this:

READY
>

This means that the computer is "ready" for you to give it instructions. On some computers, the word READY may not appear, or the prompt may be some other symbol, such as a right bracket ("]"). On a very few computers, such as the VIC-20 and the Commodore 64, there is no prompt character at all.

Following the prompt, you should see a blinking white—or black or colored—rectangle. This is called the *cursor*. On a few computers, the cursor is a short horizontal line that does not blink. The cursor indicates where the letters will appear on the video display when you type.

Yes—when you type on the computer's keyboard, the letters that you type will appear on the video screen. Try it and see. Type anything that comes to mind. Notice that the letters appear one after another on the display, as though you were typing them on a typewriter. Notice also that the cursor moves as you type, always remaining just beyond the last letter that you've placed on the screen and indicating the position where the next letter will appear.

If you should accidentally type something you didn't intend to type—if you misspelled a word, for instance—you will want to go back and correct your error. Almost every computer has a key on its keyboard that allows you to do this. Usually, this key shows an arrow pointing to the

---

Prompt—A symbol that appears on the video display of a computer indicating that the computer is expecting information from the keyboard.

Cursor—A symbol (usually a flashing white block) indicating where letters typed on the keyboard will appear on the video display.

left, or has the word BACKSPACE, DELETE (or DEL), or RUB on it. You may have to press this key in conjunction with yet another key, such as the SHIFT or CONTROL key, to make it work. On the TI-99/4A, for instance, you must press the "S" key while holding down the key marked CTRL. If your computer has none of these keys, consult the manual. When you press the right key, the cursor will move backward, erasing what you've already typed, a letter at a time. Keep pressing the key until you've erased your mistake, then type the word over again.

Now look at the right-hand side of your keyboard. There you should find a key marked RETURN or ENTER. We shall refer to it as RETURN throughout this book. Press it.

The cursor should now jump down one line and "return" to the left-hand side of the screen, just as the carriage of an electric typewriter jumps back to the left-hand margin when the carriage RETURN key is pressed. This, in fact, is why the key on your computer is marked RETURN.

Underneath what you just typed, however, the computer will probably have printed a message. It will say something like SYNTAX ERROR or ?SN ERROR or ERROR- 1. This doesn't mean that you've made a mistake; after all, you were only doing what we asked you to do. Rather, the computer is telling you that it doesn't understand what you were asking it to do. Of course, you weren't asking it to do anything at all; you were just practicing your typing. But the computer doesn't know that. The computer thinks you were trying to give it an instruction.

Whenever you see the BASIC prompt on the screen, followed by the cursor, the computer is expecting you to do something—that is, it is expecting you to give it some kind of instruction. And, because the computer has been prepared for programming in BASIC, it is expecting those instructions to be in the BASIC language.

Well, then, let's dive in headfirst and give the computer a BASIC instruction. Place your fingers on the keyboard and type the word PRINT immediately after the prompt, like this:

```
READY
>PRINT
```

Then press the RETURN key.

As before, the cursor jumps down and back to the left-hand side of the screen. This time, however, there should be no error message. If you typed the instruction properly, the computer should have no trouble understanding it.

What, you may wonder, did you ask the computer to do? Did it do it? How can you tell?

The BASIC instruction PRINT simply asks the computer to print something on the video display. Since we didn't tell it what to print, it printed a blank line. Note the blank line on the video display between the PRINT instruction and the new prompt:

```
READY
>PRINT

READY
>
```

It would be more useful if we told the computer to print something specific on its display. Type this at the prompt:

```
>PRINT "WHAT GOOD IS A COMPUTER, ANYWAY?"
```

And press the RETURN key.

Bingo! The computer prints the sentence on the screen:

```
>PRINT "WHAT GOOD IS A COMPUTER, ANYWAY?"
WHAT GOOD IS A COMPUTER, ANYWAY?
READY
>
```

The computer dutifully executes our instructions, despite the fact that we have come perilously close to insulting it. (Perhaps it's fortunate that computers don't understand English.) Notice that this sentence, as printed, no longer has quotation marks around it, even though we placed quotes in the PRINT instruction. This is because the quotes are actually part of the instruction that we gave the computer. The quotes tell the computer to print the sentence exactly as we have written it. How else might the computer print it, if not as we wrote it? We shall see, in a few pages. The quotes also tell the computer where the sentence begins and ends, so that it will not confuse it with the instructions that we are giving it. For instance, if we typed PRINT "PRINT", it would be important for the computer to understand that the first PRINT is an instruction and the second "PRINT" is simply a word that we want it to display. The quotation marks keep the computer from becoming confused.

Having the computer display sentences on the screen is fun—you might try it with a few sentences of your own, if you like—but might seem of limited usefulness, especially since the sentence is printed only once, at the moment we enter the instruction. It would be better if we could call up this same instruction at a later time and have it perform its simple task on demand, perhaps in conjunction with other instructions.

Alas, as soon as our instructions were typed and we pressed the RETURN key, the instructions were lost, consigned to electronic limbo. The computer executed—that is, performed—the instructions once, then forgot about them.

To program a computer, we must have a way for the computer to remember instructions so that it can perform them again later. We must be able to store the instructions in the computer's *memory*.

What is a computer's memory? It is a series of electronic circuits inside the computer that can store information much as you store information in your own memory, though the computer is far less likely to forget things than you are. This information is stored in the form of numbers, though it can be translated back into a form that you can understand—words, for instance. When you type information on the computer's keyboard, it is translated into a sequence of numbers and stored, however briefly, in the computer's memory.

When you typed your PRINT instruction to the computer, it was stored only long enough for the computer to translate it into action; then it was discarded. In "computerese," we can say that we typed the instructions in the *immediate*

Memory—A sequence of electronic circuits within the computer used to store information, such as programs and data, to be processed by programs.

mode—sometimes referred to as the *command mode* because we use it to "command" the computer to do something. In the immediate mode, all instructions given to the computer are executed immediately. To program the computer, we must cause the computer to retain this information for a greater length of time.

How do we do this? Actually, it's pretty simple. We merely place a number in front of our instruction, like this:

READY
>10 PRINT "THIS IS STORED IN THE COMPUTER'S MEMO-RY."

The number "10"—called a *line number* because our instruction will become a single line in a larger program— tells the computer that we are no longer working in the immediate mode but in the *programming mode*. That is, we are now writing a program. We do not want the computer to execute this instruction immediately but, rather, to store it and execute it at a later time.

Type the instruction shown above and press RETURN. You have now typed a program line. You'll notice that the command was not executed when the RETURN key was pressed. Rather, the computer has entered the program line

Immediate (command) mode—The mode in which a computer, having already been programmed to understand the BASIC language, will execute a BASIC instruction as soon as it is typed and the RETURN (or ENTER) key is pressed.

Line number—A number, typed at the left-hand margin of the video display, indicating that what follows is a line of BASIC programming, to be stored in the computer's memory.

Programming mode—The mode in which a computer, programmed to understand BASIC, will store a program line in its memory rather than executing the instructions immediately.

into its memory. To prove that the computer remembers the line, type the word LIST at the prompt, like this:

>LIST

And press RETURN. The computer will reprint your program line pretty much as you typed it. (Some computers may change your spacing slightly when reprinting a program line, though they will never tamper with words and spaces typed within quotation marks.) The instruction LIST tells the computer to reprint all program lines currently stored in its memory. You will find that this command comes in very handy when you need to reexamine a program or a portion of a program that you have typed. We will be using the LIST command many times in this book. Feel free to use it yourself, whenever you need it.

How do we get the computer to execute the instruction that we typed? Type the word RUN and press the RETURN key. You should now see the following:

>RUN
THIS LINE IS STORED IN THE COMPUTER'S MEMORY.
READY
>

The instruction RUN tells the computer to execute the program currently stored in its memory. If there is no program currently in its memory, nothing will happen. A program in BASIC is simply a collection of program lines, each containing one or more BASIC instructions. Even the simple program line that you have just typed can be considered a program; therefore, you are now a programmer. Congratulations!

Now let's add a second line to our program. Type the following:

>20 GOTO 10

And press RETURN. Now type LIST. You should see something like the following:

>LIST
10 PRINT "THIS IS STORED IN THE COMPUTER'S MEMO-
RY."

```
20 GOTO 10
READY
>
```

Notice that our first program line is still stored in the computer's memory, but now the second line has been added to it. Thus, we can write large programs simply by typing program line after program line, adding new lines to the ones that have been typed before, until we have built up a program of substantial complexity. We don't even have to type the lines in order, as we shall see.

What does our new program instruction do? There's an easy way to find out. Type RUN and press RETURN.

Actually, this program does quite a bit—or at least it seems to. You should now see the sentence THIS IS STORED IN THE COMPUTER'S MEMORY being printed over and over on the video display. To see how the program works, type LIST and . . .

What? Nothing happens when you type? Indeed, there's a slight problem here. The program doesn't want to stop executing. Nothing will happen when you try to type on the keyboard.

The bad news is that this program has every intention of executing forever, or until someone turns the computer off or the machine falls apart from old age, whichever comes first. Furthermore, while the program is executing, the keyboard is "locked out"; that is, we can bang—gently, of course—on the keys all day without the computer paying the least bit of attention. This will happen during the execution of most programs. Except in the few special cases, which we will look at in a moment, the computer automatically locks out the keyboard while a program is being executed.

The good news is that not every key on the keyboard is frozen out. One remains alive. On most small computers it is called BREAK. On a few it is called RUN-STOP. On the Apple, you must press the "C" key while holding down the key marked CTRL. On the TI-99/4A you must press the "4" key while holding down the CTRL key.

This key, which we will refer to from now on as the BREAK key, interrupts the program in progress and returns you to the immediate mode. Press it. The prompt and the cursor should now appear on the screen again.

Type LIST. Your program should look like this:

```
>LIST
10 PRINT "THIS IS STORED IN THE COMPUTER'S MEMO-
RY."
20 GOTO 10
```

In fact, it looks pretty much like it did before; nothing has changed while it was running. How does it work?

We know what the instruction in line 10 does. Can you guess what the instruction in line 20 does?

If you guessed that it tells the computer to go back and execute the instruction in line 10 again, go to (GOTO?) the head of the class. That's exactly what it does. The GOTO statement tells the computer to "go to" the specified program line—in this case, line 10—and execute the instructions it finds there plus all the instructions in the lines following. Thus, the computer is forced to repeat the instruction in line 10 again and again, because every time it finishes executing it, line 20 tells it to go back and do it again, *ad infinitum.*

As a rule, the instructions in a computer program execute in order of their line numbers. The GOTO statement is used when you want to change the order in which the program executes, as we did above.

What if we wrote an instruction telling the computer to go to a line number that wasn't in the program? The computer would resent our playing tricks on it and would give us an error message, that's what.

Before we go on to more advanced programs than this, there are a couple of other things that you should note in relation to typing in program lines. Type the following:

```
15 PRINT "ON WITH THE SHOW . . ."
```

And press RETURN. Now type LIST. You should see the following:

```
10 PRINT "THIS IS STORED IN THE COMPUTER'S MEMO-
RY."
15 PRINT "ON WITH THE SHOW . . ."
20 GOTO 10
```

Our new program line has been inserted neatly between the previous two. This is an important point to remember. We don't have to type the lines of a program in order. The computer automatically sorts the lines into numerical order according to line number. Thus, line 15 is inserted between lines 10 and 20, though it was typed after the other two lines.

How do we remove lines that we don't need? Type the number 20 at the prompt and press RETURN. Now list the program. Line 20 should be gone. This is all you need to do to remove an unwanted program line: Type the number of the line you wish to remove and press RETURN, without typing anything on the line. The computer will remove the old line without inserting a new one.

Some computers also have a DELETE instruction. Type the following:

>DELETE 10

And press RETURN. If you got an error message when you typed that, your computer lacks the DELETE instruction. If you didn't get an error message, list your program. Line 10 should be gone. The DELETE command, if your computer has it, can also be used to delete more than one line at a time, which is useful if you want to remove a large number of program lines. (It's certainly a lot faster than deleting them one by one.) For instance, the instruction DELETE 100-500 will delete all the lines between and including 100 and 500. The DELETE command should only be used in the immediate mode, though some computers may allow you to include it in a program line. You might check the manual to be certain of the way in which your computer uses the DELETE instruction. If your computer doesn't have the DELETE command, check to see if it has another instruction that does the same thing.

To remove an entire program from the computer's memory and prepare the computer to accept a new program, you simply type the word NEW. In fact, it is a good idea to type NEW whenever you wish to begin writing a program.

Now you've learned to type a program. In the next chapter, we'll give you quite a few new computer instructions to type.

Suggested Projects

The remaining chapters of this book will each end with a section entitled SUGGESTED PROJECTS. In it, you will find a number of suggested programming ideas and experiments that you might want to try on your computer. The actual creation of the programs will be up to you; if you have studied the preceding chapter and tried the examples included in each, you should have all the information necessary to write the programs. Because each programmer will approach the job of programming in a different way, there are no right or wrong ways of writing these programs; thus, you will not find any "answers" to these programming projects at the back of this book. If the program works when you try it on a computer, then you'll know you got it right; if it doesn't, then keep making changes until it does. These projects are mostly for your enjoyment, but they will also help you to sharpen your growing skills as a programmer. The best way to learn programming is by doing just that—programming. And although programming is a valuable skill to acquire, it is the belief of the author of this book that it is also a great deal of fun.

1. The PRINT statement is very powerful and can be used to display a great many different things on the computer's video screen, as we shall see in subsequent chapters. Experiment with this command. Use it to print various words and sentences on the

computer's screen. Try leaving off the quotation marks from the sentences to see what happens. On most computers, this will not cause an error message but will produce an odd result. We will explain why this happens in a later chapter.

2. Write a program that combines a PRINT statement and a GOTO statement, your object being to print the same word or sentence repeatedly on the screen. Remember to place the word or sentence in quotes. Run the program. Now, rewrite the PRINT statement so that there is a semicolon (";") following the word or sentence to be printed. Make sure that the semicolon comes after the last quotation mark—that is, make sure it does not fall within the quotes. Run the program again. How is it different this time? What did the semicolon do? We will look at this process in more detail in a later chapter.

3

A VERY
EXPENSIVE
CALCULATOR

We have now dipped our toes into a tiny corner of the vast sea of computer programming. Before we trust ourselves completely to the waves, let's backtrack and look more closely at one of the BASIC instructions introduced in the last chapter, the PRINT instruction.

The PRINT instruction is one of the most versatile—and valuable—commands in BASIC. We can use it in a large number of ways.

Type the following at the prompt:

>PRINT 42

And press RETURN. You should see something that looks like this:

>PRINT 42
42

The computer simply printed the number 42 on the screen. The following instructions also print numbers on the screen:

PRINT 317
PRINT 4
PRINT 192632
PRINT −14.36

You can experiment with printing other numbers, if you like. Numbers larger than about 1,000,000 will be printed in a rather odd fashion, called *exponential notation.* Extremely large numbers will not be printed at all, and will cause the computer to give you an error message, something along the lines of OVERFLOW ERROR or ?OV ERROR. Be sure not to include any punctuation in your numbers other than a single decimal point (".") if needed. Commas, for instance (as in 1,000,000), will only confuse the computer. So will having more than one decimal point or a dollar sign.

You'll notice that we don't have to put quotation marks around numbers, as we did with the sentences we printed in the last chapter. The computer is quite capable of recognizing a number and will not confuse it with a BASIC instruction or anything else. If we want to, however, we can enclose the numbers in quotes before printing them, like this:

PRINT "4004"
PRINT "688107"
PRINT "1.1111111"

This will produce the same result as printing a number without quotes.

What's the difference between printing a number with and without quotes? One difference is that the quotation marks allow us to include punctuation marks and other characters (letters or symbols) in a number, like this:

PRINT "2,467,800"
PRINT "$44.98"
PRINT "44 DOLLARS AND 98 CENTS"

All these instructions would be considered illegal by the computer if they were not enclosed within quotation marks.

The main difference between numbers inside quotes and numbers without quotes, however, is in what we can

---

Exponential notation—A method of writing large numbers; sometimes called floating point notation.

do with the numbers. Numbers that are not enclosed within quotes, for instance, can have arithmetic performed on them by the computer, as though the computer were a very expensive electronic calculator.

To see the computer add two numbers together, type the following:

>PRINT 4 + 7

And press RETURN. The computer should respond like this:

>PRINT 4 + 7
11

Instead of printing the numbers exactly as you typed them, the computer adds the two numbers and prints their sum! A handy trick, indeed. On the other hand, if you want the computer to print exactly what you've written, you type it like this:

>PRINT "4 + 7"

And press RETURN. The computer will respond like this:

>PRINT "4 + 7"
4 + 7

Because the computer handles symbols inside quotation marks very differently from the way it handles symbols outside quotation marks, we have special terms for these two different methods of handling symbols.

A collection of symbols—numbers, letters, punctuation marks, whatever—inside quotation marks is called a *string*. The following are all strings:

String—A sequence of alphanumeric characters—letters, numerals, punctuation marks, special symbols, etc.

"THIS IS A STRING"
"4,682,708,961.333333"
"(&$%!@#9@*:%)'*&"
"E4E4E4E4E4E4E4"
"JOHN Q. DOE"

We can use the PRINT command to display any string of characters we want on the screen, though most versions of BASIC place a restriction on the maximum allowable length of a single string. This is usually 255 characters, though it is sometimes less. However, we must always place the string within quotation marks.

A number outside quotation marks is called a *numeric value*—or, more simply, a *number*. The following are numbers:

1.4387921
468
963788
5
−3469.7

As we saw a moment ago, we can perform addition on numbers. Let's look at some of the other arithmetic operations we can perform on numbers.

If we can perform addition with a computer, it makes sense that we can also perform subtraction. And so we can. Type this:

PRINT 24 − 6

And press RETURN. The computer will print the number 18 on the screen. As it did with addition, the computer performed the subtraction and printed the result.

We use the asterisk ("*") to perform multiplication. This may seem odd, since we ordinarily use the symbol "X" to perform multiplication. However, the computer might mistake the "X" for something altogether different, as we shall see in the next chapter. To perform multiplication, type the following:

Numeric value—Simply, a number.

PRINT 4 * 9

And press RETURN. The computer will respond with the number 36, which is 4 times 9.

Division is performed with the slash ("/") symbol. Type this:

PRINT 9 / 3

And press RETURN. The computer will respond with the number 3, which is 9 divided by 3.

Because these symbols ("+," "−," "*," and "/") perform arithmetic operations, we usually refer to them as *arithmetic operators*.

To make sure you understand how to perform arithmetic on a computer, type the following as an exercise:

```
10 PRINT 4 + 119
20 PRINT 13 / 7
30 PRINT 15 * 64 / 1.78
40 PRINT 1 + 2 + 3 + 4
50 PRINT 7 + 8 − 17
```

Run the program to see the computer execute these various operations.

Notice that we can combine various arithmetic operations together in a single PRINT statement, one after another. It's important, however, that we say a few words about the order in which the computer will perform these operations. Although the computer will normally perform arithmetic operations in the order in which it finds them, it will perform all multiplication and division operations *before* it performs additions and subtractions. That is, it will perform all the multiplications and divisions in your statement in the order in which it finds them and then proceed to perform the additions and subtractions in the order that it finds them.

Arithmetic operator—A symbol representing an arithmetic operation, such as addition, multiplication, etc. The major arithmetic operators in BASIC can be found in the BASIC Vocabulary section of this book.

In the operation 2 + 4 * 6, for instance, the computer will multiply 4 times 6, then add the answer, which will be 24, to the number 2, obtaining a result of 26. If you want to change the order in which the computer performs operations, you can use parentheses. Putting parentheses around an operation causes the computer to perform that operation first. If we wrote (2 + 4) * 6, for instance, the computer would add 2 and 4, then multiply the result by 6. If more than one operation is enclosed in parentheses, then those operations are performed in order.

Look at the following operations and see if you can figure out the order the computer uses to perform the operations. To verify your result, do the operations yourself, write the answers on paper, then try printing them on the computer to see if it gets the same answers:

4 * 8 + 8 / 2
3 − 4 / 2
(4 + 7) * (8 / 4)
15 / (6 − 5 * 3) + 11

We can even put parentheses inside parentheses, like this:

2 * (8 / (7 − 5))

The computer will solve the problem from the inside out; that is, it will solve the operation(s) in the innermost set of parentheses first, then work its way outward. In this example, the computer would subtract 5 from 7, obtaining a result of 2, then divide 8 by the result, which would produce an answer of 4. Then it would multiply the 4 by 2 for a final answer of 8.

In this book we won't worry too much about fancy use of parentheses, though you should know how they work in case you run into them in a program sometime or need them for a program of your own. If you've taken a course in algebra, you've probably already encountered them and have a pretty good understanding of how computers perform arithmetic.

Obviously, we can't perform arithmetic on strings, since a statement like PRINT "APPLES" * "ORANGES" would make little sense. However, there is an arithmetic-like operation that we can perform on strings. It is called *concatenation,* and, like addition, it is performed with the plus sign ("+"). (On the TI-99/4 and TI-99/4A, concatenation is performed with the ampersand ["&"]. On the Atari computers, concatenation cannot be performed in the normal manner.)

Concatenation simply means creating a large string out of two or more smaller strings. To see how it works, type this:

>PRINT "LIGHT" + "HOUSE"

And press RETURN. (If you are using a TI computer, substitute the ampersand for the plus sign, like this: PRINT "LIGHT" & "HOUSE".) The computer should respond like this:

>PRINT "LIGHT" + "HOUSE"
LIGHTHOUSE

The computer concatenates the two smaller strings "light" and "house" into one large string: "lighthouse." You can concatenate any two strings you like, simply by placing a plus sign in between them and printing them on the video display. Be careful, however, that the plus sign does not accidentally fall within the quotation marks. If it does, the computer will mistake it for part of the string that you are asking it to print, like this:

>PRINT "LIGHT + HOUSE"
LIGHT + HOUSE

Although the computer's ability to perform arithmetic and arithmeticlike operations is certainly useful, it does little to set the computer apart from, say, a pocket calculator, or even an abacus. The real strength of a computer becomes apparent only when we combine everything we've learned in the last two chapters with variables, the subject of the next chapter.

Concatenation—The linking together of more than one string to form a single, larger string.

Suggested Projects

1. The value of using a computer to solve arithmetic problems should be obvious. It is important, however, that you understand how to translate ordinary arithmetic, using ordinary arithmetic terms, into a form that the computer can understand. For the most part, this is simple enough, because most of the symbols used for arithmetic problems in the BASIC language are the same ones you learned in math class when you were younger, though you must remember to use the asterisk for multiplication. If you are currently taking a class in mathematics, or have access to a mathematics textbook, it would be a good idea to translate some of the problems from that text into BASIC. Type them as PRINT statements on your computer, and see if the answer agrees with the one you obtain by using pencil and paper.

2. Imagine that you are running a small business, say, selling flowers on a street corner. You are selling three different kinds of flowers: roses, carnations, and daisies. Roses sell for $21.95 a dozen, carnations for $10.95 a dozen, and daisies for $8.49 a dozen. Write a PRINT statement that will tell you how much you have earned if you have sold 44 dozen roses, 33 dozen carnations, and 22 dozen daisies. (The answer to the problem, incidentally, is $1,513.93. Now see if you can make the computer produce the same answer.)

3. Write a PRINT statement to solve the problem 3 + 1 * 4 − 7 / 2. Can you tell in which order the computer will perform these arithmetic operations? Can you rewrite the PRINT statement, using parentheses, so that the computer will perform the addition first? The subtraction? The division? Can you rewrite it so that the division will be solved first, followed by the subtraction, then the addition, and finally the multiplication? Can you rewrite it so that the subtraction is solved first, then the multiplication, then the division, then the addition? Try writing a PRINT statement for every possible order in which these operations can be performed. Try doing it without changing the order in which the operations appear.

4. This book is being written with the aid of a word processor—that is, a computer programmed to behave like a fancy typewriter. When I press a certain button on the computer, it tells me how many characters there are in the chapter that I am typing. The computer tells me (at the time of this writing) that this chapter is 13,302 characters long. (It counts letters, punctuation marks, numbers, and blank spaces as characters.) Assume that the average word is 6 characters long (including the spaces between words). Assume further that the average page in this book is 250 words long. Write a PRINT statement to calculate how many words there are in this chapter and a second PRINT statement to calculate how many pages these words will occupy. Then count the number of pages in this chapter and see if the figures agree. If they don't, write a PRINT statement that will calculate the actual number of words on a page, assuming that the figure of 6 characters per word is correct and that there are 13,302 characters in this chapter. Count the number of words on an actual page and see if the figures are similar. They probably won't agree precisely, because no one page is likely to have exactly the number of words found on an average page.

4
THE POWER
OF VARIABLES

If you've studied mathematics, especially algebra, you've already run into the concept of *variables*. If you haven't, don't worry—we'll explain them as we go along. But even if you already know about variables, you should still pay careful attention. Computer variables don't always behave like the ones that come up in algebra class.

What is a variable? It is a symbol—generally a letter or a letter combined with other letters, numbers, punctuation marks, and so on—that can represent, or stand for, a number or other symbols.

Well, that definition may be a little confusing, so let's define by example. Type the following:

LET A = 3

And press RETURN.

Nothing should happen—nothing visible, anyway. Now type this:

>PRINT A

And press RETURN. (No quotation marks around the letter A, please.) The computer should do this:

Variable—A word or identifier used to stand for a location in the computer's memory at which a value is stored. Stored values may be changed in the course of a program.

>PRINT A
3

Instead of printing the letter A, the computer prints the number 3. The computer shouldn't print the letter A literally as we typed it, of course, because it has no quotation marks around it. But why does it print the number 3?

The letter A is a variable. In fact, whenever a letter of the alphabet appears on the screen without quotes around it, the computer assumes that the letter is a variable, or the first character in the name of a variable. This is why we must put quotes around all alphabetical strings, so that the computer will not mistake them for variables. (This is also the reason we cannot use the letter "X" as the symbol for multiplication.)

When we typed LET A = 3 we were telling the computer to set the variable A equal to the number 3—that is, to allow A to "stand in" for, or represent, the number 3. From then on, whenever we make reference to the variable A in an instruction to the computer, it will treat it as though it actually were the number 3.

For instance, type this:

>PRINT A + 7

The computer should respond with the number 10, which is 3 plus 7.

Now type this:

>PRINT A * 21

The computer should respond with the number 63, which is 3 times 21.

Now type this:

>LET B = 14

This introduces a new variable, B, and sets it equal to the number 14.

Now type this:

>PRINT A + B

[33]

The computer should respond with the number 17, which is 3 plus 14. It is now treating the variables A and B as though they were the numbers 3 and 14, respectively.

In the example just given, the variables A and B are acting as *numeric variables* because they are being used to represent numeric values—that is, numbers. On most computers, numeric variables are represented by one or two letters or a letter followed by a number. The following are typical numeric variables:

AB
V1
HP
M9

Most computers will allow you to use longer variable names than this—that is, variable names longer than two letters—but the computer will only look at the first two letters of the name. Thus, NULL, NUMBER, NUTMEG and NU7000 would all be valid variable names, but the computer would treat them as though they were all the same variable with the name NU. Notable exceptions to this rule are the Atari computers, which can recognize different variable names up to 128 characters in length, and the TI-99/4 and 99/4A, which can identify different variable names up to 15 characters in length.

Another way of looking at a variable is as a label representing a place in the computer's memory, a kind of cubbyhole with a name, if you will. When we tell the computer to LET A = 3, we are actually telling it to store the number 3 in the location—the cubbyhole—that we have labeled A. When we then tell the computer to PRINT A, we are telling it to go to location A, find the number that is stored there, and print it on the video display. PRINT A + 17 retrieves the number from location A, adds it to 17, and prints the result on the screen. In the same way, LET B = 14 establishes a cubbyhole called B and stores the number 14 there.

Numeric variable—A variable that may be assigned numeric values.

The phrase LET (variable name) = (number) is called an *assignment statement* because it assigns a value to a variable. On most small computers, with the conspicuous exception of the Timex Sinclair, the word LET is optional; you don't have to use it if you don't want to. Instead, you may simply write A = 3, to use just one example. There are some experts who feel that the use of the word LET makes the meaning of the program clearer; however, the decision to use it is left to the individual programmer. Nonetheless, to avoid possible confusion, we will continue using LET in this book.

We can do any number of things with numeric variables. We may, for instance, set a variable equal to the result of an arithmetic operation, as in these assignment statements:

```
LET X = 4 * 3
LET HY = 12 / 4
LET BB = 62 + 8 / 17 * 6
```

We can even set variables equal to other variables, like this:

```
LET A = B
LET C1 = C1 + 2
LET AA = B * C
LET BX = H + 3 / J
```

Remember: Once the computer has set a variable equal to a number, be that number the result of an arithmetic operation on the value of another variable or whatever, the computer will treat that variable from then on as though it *were* that number, until we choose to alter the value of the variable. This, in fact, is one of the most valuable things about variables and is why they are called variables. Their values can change again and again in the course of the program. The following program demonstrates this:

Assignment statement—An instruction to the computer to assign a specific value to a variable.

```
10 LET A = 5
20 PRINT A
30 LET A = 19 / 7
40 PRINT A
50 LET A = 2001 + 4
60 PRINT A
70 LET A = A + 1
80 PRINT A
```

This program simply assigns and reassigns values to the variable A, then prints out those values. Each time the value of A is printed, it is different; it has been altered since the last PRINT statement. Notice that the final assignment statement, in line 70, sets A equal to itself plus 1. How is it possible, in effect, to set a number equal to itself? The answer is that the computer performs the arithmetic part of this instruction before it performs the assignment part. It retrieves the value currently at the location labeled A, adds it to 1, and only then stores the result back at location A.

Numeric variables are not the only kind of variable that your computer recognizes. There exists yet another kind of variable known as a *string variable*—a variable that can be set equal to a string!

String variables have names much like those of numeric variables, except that string variable names must end with the symbol "$". Though this symbol looks a great deal like a dollar sign—and, in fact, is a dollar sign—BASIC programmers often refer to it simply as "string." An example of a string variable would be A$ (pronounced "A-string"). Some other possible string variables would be:

FG$ ("F-G-string")
H$ ("H-string")
WO$ ("W-O-string")
X1$ ("X-1-string")

How do we use string variables? Much as we use numeric

String Variable—A variable that may be assigned string values.

variables. An assignment statement for a string variable might look like this:

LET A$ = "HELLO"

Try typing that line in the immediate mode, then type this:

PRINT A$

And press RETURN. Your computer should respond like this:

>PRINT A$
HELLO

Just as the computer treats a numeric variable as though it were the number we have set it equal to, so the computer treats a string variable as though it were the string we have set it equal to. In that last example, the computer treated the string variable A$ as though it were the string "HEL-LO".

The following are all legitimate assignment statements for string variables:

LET ZX$ = "HOME COMPUTER"
LET Y$ = "BULK" + "HEAD"
LET PR$ = A$
LET L$ = ZZ$ + AA$
LET MN$ = P$ + "GOODBYE"

And so forth. Notice that we can set string variables equal to other string variables, concatenated strings, and even concatenated string variables. Although we can't perform subtraction, multiplication, or division on string variables, most versions of BASIC offer a number of arithmeticlike operations that can be performed on string variables.

If you are using an Atari computer, by now you may have noticed that string variables do not behave in quite the manner that we have advertised. This is because the Atari handles string variables in a way that is rather unique. It is necessary, on the Atari, to announce, preferably somewhere near the beginning of a program, the names of all the string variables that you intend to use in that program and the maximum length of the strings that you will be setting those variables equal to. This announcement must be made with a DIM statement. The word DIM is short for "dimension"; the DIM statement is used to tell the computer the "dimensions" of the strings that you will be working with. For instance, if you decide to use a string variable called A$, and you think that A$ may, in the course of your program, be set equal to a string ninety characters in length, you must dimension A$ to a length of 90. This means that, sometime before you first try to set A$ equal to a string, you must write the following instruction in your program or in the immediate mode if that's what you're currently working in: DIM A$ (90). This tells the computer that you will be using a variable called A$ and that it will be set equal to strings up to ninety characters in length. We may also set it equal to *shorter* strings in the course of the program, but the *maximum* string length will be ninety characters.

It's okay to overestimate the length of the longest string you will be using, but don't overdo it, because the computer will set aside valuable computer memory for storing those strings, memory you could be using to write larger programs. You may even dimension more than one string variable in a single statement. Two string variables could be dimensioned together like this: DIM A$ (100), NAME$ (150). Now, if you wish to go back and try the examples again, you may do so. Just be sure that you type the name of the string variable in a dimension statement before using it in an assignment statement. Once again, this is only necessary if you are using an Atari computer. We will not be including DIM statements in the programs in this book, so Atari owners will have to add them to the beginning of any programs that contain strings. The DIM statement has a quite different meaning on other computers, though we will not be covering its use in this book.

Are you confident now that you understand what variables are and how they work? If not, you might trying glancing over this chapter one more time, because variables may well be the most important concept that we will study in this book—and possibly the most important concept in all of computing.

If you're ready, though, let's plunge ahead into the next chapter, where we will learn, among other things, a way to interact with our programs while they are actually running—and really make our programs come to life!

Suggested Projects

1. Go back to the projects at the end of the last chapter and try to solve them with the aid of variables. You need only to substitute assignment statements for the PRINT statements that you originally used and then ask the computer to print the value of the variable. For instance, the statement PRINT 44 * 21.95 + 33 * 10.95 + 22 * 8.49—which is a possible solution to the problem of the flowers in Chapter Three—could be rewritten like this:

```
10 LET IN = 44 * 21.95 + 33 * 10.95 + 22 * 8.49
20 PRINT IN
```

This program sets the variable IN equal to the amount of income that we have derived from the sale of the flowers, then prints this value of the variable IN. Try solving the other projects in this same manner.

*2. Is it possible to set a string variable equal to a number? Try it and see. If the computer refuses to accept your instruction, try rewriting it. (Hint: In an earlier chapter, we printed numbers as strings. How was this done?) What happens if we try to "add" these string variables together? Is it the same thing that happens when we add numeric variables together?

3. We saw in this chapter how it is possible to set a variable equal to itself plus another number; for instance, LET A = A + 1. This sets A equal to a num-

ber that is one greater than the number to which it was previously equal. The assignment statement LET A = A + 2 would assign A a new value, equal to the old value plus 2. Write a program that combines such an assignment statement with a GOTO statement and a PRINT statement, to print a sequence of numbers such as 0, 1, 2, 3, 4, 5, 6, 7, and so on. (Hint: Begin by assigning the value of 0 to the variable, then print the value of the variable, add 1 to it, and go back to the line that prints the value of the variable with a GOTO statement. You will have to end this program by hitting the BREAK key.) Try rewriting the program to print the sequence 0, 2, 4, 6, 8, 10, 12 . . . , then the sequence 0, 3, 6, 9, 12, 15, 18 . . . .

THE THINKING COMPUTER

It's easy enough to set a variable equal to a number or a string. We simply type LET followed by the variable name, then an equals sign followed by the number or string we want to set the variable equal to.

But, truth to tell, we are not always going to know, as we type our program, what it is we want the variable to equal.

It would be convenient if we could write our programs in such a way that the user of the program, rather than the programmer, can change the value of the variables in the program while the program is actually running. (We are defining the word user here to mean the person who actually runs the program. Throughout this book you will probably play the roles of both programmer and user, unless you invite a friend or a member of your family to run the programs you have typed or written.)

There is, in fact, a way that this can be done. It is the INPUT statement. It cannot be used in the immediate mode, however; we must type it into a program.

Type the following program:

```
10 PRINT "TYPE A NUMBER"
20 INPUT A
30 PRINT A
```

And run it. The computer should respond like this:

```
>RUN
TYPE A NUMBER
?
```

What the computer has done, apparently, is to print the sentence you asked it to, followed by a question mark on the next line. How odd. Where did this question mark come from? And directly after the question mark you should see a blinking cursor.

This is odder still! You may recall from an earlier chapter that a blinking cursor means that the computer is prepared to accept input from the keyboard, but you'll also recall that the computer tends to lock up its keyboard during the execution of a program. And, whether you're aware of it or not, our program is still executing.

This is the magic of the INPUT statement. It unlocks the keyboard while the program is running and allows you to type, just as you would while writing a program.

Try typing a number, as requested. The number should appear on the video display as you type it. Do not insert any punctuation into the number—except, perhaps, for a decimal point.

Press RETURN. The video display should now look something like this:

```
? 1487
1487
```

The number that you typed was printed on the line beneath your input. Why?

List the program. Read it. Notice that line 10 says INPUT A. As we just noted, the INPUT statement unlocks the keyboard and allows you to type. In this case, you typed a number. What does the letter A following the INPUT command mean? A is a variable, just like the ones we studied in the last chapter. When you type a number from the keyboard and press RETURN, the INPUT command sets the variable A equal to the number you typed. If you typed the number 1487, the variable A should now be equal to 1487.

Then, in line 20, where the program asks the computer to print the value of variable A on the video display, it prints the number 1487, or whatever number you actually typed in. Simple?

To put it another way, the INPUT statement is a kind of assignment statement. It assigns to the specified variable the value that you type in while the program is actually running.

Incidentally, as you have probably already noticed, the INPUT command automatically prints a question mark on the screen. This is called the *input prompt*. It simply indicates to the user that the computer is ready for input. Of course, the blinking cursor indicates this as well.

Run the program again. This time type a word or a letter in response to the input prompt, rather than a number, and press RETURN. The computer will respond with a comment such as REDO or REDO FROM START, followed by another prompt. This means that you have responded with the wrong kind of input and are being given a second chance to get it right. The computer expected a number and you gave it a string.

Now type a number and press RETURN. The computer will give the proper response.

Why does the computer expect a number and not a string? List the program. Look at line 20. Notice that the variable following the INPUT command is a numeric variable, not a string variable. This tells the computer that it is going to receive numeric input. When the computer is prepared for numeric input, it will accept nothing else.

Can we make the INPUT command accept string input? Sure we can. Let's change our current program to the following:

```
10 PRINT "TYPE A WORD"
20 INPUT A$
30 PRINT A$
```

The only major change that we have made to the program, other than altering the sentence printed by line 10, is to substitute string variables for the numeric ones in lines 20 and 30. This tells the computer to expect string input from the keyboard.

Input prompt—The prompt, usually a question mark, displayed by the computer when the INPUT command is executed.

Run the program. Type a word in response to the input prompt. Press RETURN. (It is not necessary in this case to place quotation marks around the word.)

If you typed the word HELLO in response to the prompt, your video display will now look like this:

```
? HELLO
HELLO
```

Much as before, the INPUT command accepted the string HELLO from the keyboard, then set A$ equal to it. In line 30, the computer printed the value of A$ on the screen.

If we type a number in response to this input prompt, will we get another REDO message, because the computer is expecting string input? No. The computer is quite happy to accept a number as a string, just as it will accept any other collection of characters and symbols as a string. However, when we set a string variable equal to a number, we lose the ability to perform arithmetic on that number, since we cannot perform arithmetic on strings.

To see one possible use to which we can put the INPUT command, type this program:

```
10 PRINT "WHAT IS YOUR NAME";
20 INPUT A$
30 PRINT "NICE TO SEE YOU,   ";A$
40 GOTO 10
```

Run it. The first thing you will notice is a slight change in the input prompt. Your screen should look like this:

```
WHAT IS YOUR NAME?
```

The input prompt is no longer underneath the sentence; it is now immediately after it, just like an ordinary question mark. Note that we did not put a question mark at the end of the sentence in line 10 of the program, even though this sentence is obviously a question. We didn't need a question mark; the INPUT command supplied it for us.

But why does the question mark appear at the end of the sentence rather than on the next line, as before? Ordinarily, when we print a sentence on the screen (or anything else) with the PRINT command, the computer automatically prints a carriage return at the end of whatever was printed. A carriage return, you'll recall, is when the cursor—or the position where the next character is being printed on the computer's screen—drops to the next line and returns to the left-hand margin, just as when you hit the carriage RETURN key on an electric typewriter or throw the carriage return lever on a manual typewriter. At the end of the sentence in line 10, however, we have placed a semicolon. It is put after the closing quote, so that the computer will not mistake it for part of the string. The semicolon tells the computer not to put into effect the carriage return, so that the next item printed on the screen—in this case, the input prompt—is printed directly after the sentence, there being no carriage return to move the print position back to the left margin. Instead, the print position remains right where it was left after the PRINT statement, just as the print head of a typewriter remains where we leave it until we deliberately tell it to move.

The use of the semicolon is a handy programming trick, and you are encouraged to remember it. In fact, if you attempted project #2 in Chapter Two, you have already seen the semicolon in action.

At the end of the sentence, after the question mark, is a flashing cursor, indicating that the computer is waiting for input. Since the sentence asks you to type your name, do as it says. If your name is Paul, the computer will respond something like this:

WHAT IS YOUR NAME? PAUL
NICE TO SEE YOU, PAUL.

This is a clever, though simple, trick to play on a friend, since it makes it seem as though the computer is able to learn someone's name—which, in a sense, it is. If you look back at the program, you'll see that we did this by printing the sentence NICE TO SEE YOU, , followed directly by the variable A$, which by that time had been set equal to your name by the INPUT statement. Notice that the sentence we printed has a blank space directly after the comma and before the closing quote. The computer treats this blank space as though it were part of the string. This allows a space to be printed between the comma and "Paul"; otherwise, the computer would print A$ directly after the comma, and the sentence would look like this: NICE TO SEE YOU,PAUL.

You'll notice that immediately after the computer greets you by name, it asks for your name again. This is because of the statement GOTO 10 in line 40. This causes the computer to return to the beginning of the program and begin executing it again.

We did this to give you a chance to experiment repeatedly with answering the input prompt. Try typing various responses, even meaningless gibberish. The computer will treat them all the same, since it has no idea of what these strings actually mean.

When a program is designed in such a way that the computer repeatedly executes the same series of statements, as this program is, we say that the computer is executing a *loop,* so named because the computer almost seems to be going in circles. Loops are very important, if only because they can make relatively short programs behave as though they were longer ones. This program, for instance, is only four lines long, but it will run forever if we let it.

To end this program, we must strike the BREAK key or its equivalent. (We listed some equivalents to the BREAK key back in Chapter Two.) If you have a Commodore computer, you may have to press both the RUN-STOP and RESTORE keys simultaneously. This is because Commodore computers are very reluctant to exit a program in the middle of an INPUT statement, for some obscure reason of their own. On the other hand, some Commodore computers will break out of an INPUT statement automatically if you simply press RETURN in response to the input prompt, without typing anything first.

Now let's turn that last program into something a little more sophisticated. Add these lines to the program, replacing the name *Paul* in the listing with your own name:

Loop—A section of a program that is executed more than once in the course of a single program run.

```
30 IF A$ = "PAUL" THEN PRINT "HELLO,  " A$:GOTO 10
40 PRINT "YOUR NAME IS "A$"? WHAT HAPPENED TO
PAUL?"
50 GOTO 10
```

Be sure you put the quotation marks in the right places, so that the computer can identify the variables properly.

What's going on in the above program? Run it and see. When the computer asks your name, respond honestly at first, with the name that you used in the program, then make up a different name and see how the computer responds.

The result should be something like this:

```
WHAT IS YOUR NAME? PAUL
HELLO, PAUL
WHAT IS YOUR NAME? GEORGE
YOUR NAME IS GEORGE? WHAT HAPPENED TO PAUL?
WHAT IS YOUR NAME? RUMPELSTILTSKIN
YOUR NAME IS RUMPELSTILTSKIN? WHAT HAPPENED TO
PAUL?
WHAT IS YOUR NAME? PAUL
HELLO, PAUL
```

And so forth. Since the computer will ask the question again and again until you stop it, you can experiment with dozens of possible names. However, by now you probably have caught on to what is happening: The computer will respond HELLO only if the name you give it is Paul or whatever name you used in the program.

How does it work? If you look closely at the program you may find that it is almost self-explanatory. The instruction in line 30 says IF A$ = "PAUL" THEN PRINT "HELLO, "A$. Obviously, this defines the specific way in which the computer is to respond, *as long as the name you give it is Paul!* If the name you give it is *not* Paul, it responds with the instructions on line 40 instead.

This sort of programming technique is called an IF-THEN statement. Next to the ability to use variables, IF-THEN statements, and their equivalents in other programming languages, are the most powerful capability that computers have. Such an instruction allows the computer to make a decision based on external, or internal, events—in this case, your choice of what name to type on the keyboard. You can actually control the functioning of the program while it is running by choosing to type or not type the name Paul or whatever.

An IF-THEN statement generally takes this form: the word IF, followed by a condition that may or may not be true, followed by the word THEN, followed by an instruction. In our current program, A$ = "PAUL" is the condition. This is true or not true, depending on what name you type in response to the input prompt. The computer examines this statement, deciding whether or not it is true. If the condition is true—that is, if A$ is indeed equal to PAUL—the computer then looks to the instruction following the word THEN and executes it. In this case, that instruction is PRINT "HELLO, "A$. On the other hand, if the condition is not true—that is, if A$ is not equal to PAUL—then it ignores the instruction following the word THEN and jumps immediately to the next line of the program.

You may have already noticed something odd about line 30. Following the instruction PRINT "HELLO, "A$ there is yet another instruction, separated from the first by a colon (":"). It is permissible in most versions of BASIC to put more than one instruction on a single program line, although we have not done so until now. These instructions must be separated from one another by a colon, however. A program line with more than one instruction on it is called a *multi-statement line*. When you place an IF-THEN statement on a multi-statement line, every instruction following the word THEN is contingent on the IF condition. That is, if the condition following the word IF is not true, the computer will ignore *all* remaining instructions on the line. In our program here we have included the instruction GOTO 10 after the IF-THEN statement so that when the IF condition is true the computer will not proceed to execute the instruc-

---

Multi-statement line—A line of a BASIC program that contains more than one program statement; statements in a multi-statement line are usually separated by colons.

tions on line 40 but will return and begin executing instructions on line 10 once more.

If you are using a Timex Sinclair 1000 or a TI-99/4A with TI BASIC, you may have already discovered that your computer will not allow you to type the preceding program as it was written here. Sorry. Sinclair 1000 BASIC and TI BASIC do not allow multi-statement lines. To write an IF-THEN statement like this in Sinclair or TI BASIC, it is usually necessary to place a GOTO statement directly after the word THEN so that the program will branch to a line containing the rest of the routine you want it to perform, which can then be on several consecutive lines if there are several consecutive operations to be performed. For example, we could rewrite the last three lines of our program, using no multi-statement lines, like this:

```
30 IF A$ = "PAUL" THEN GOTO 60
40 PRINT "YOUR NAME IS  "A$"? WHAT HAPPENED TO
PAUL?"
50 GOTO 10
60 PRINT "HELLO,  "A$
70 GOTO 10
```

If you follow the flow of this program by hand—that is, without running it on your computer—you will see that the instructions on lines 60 and 70 will execute only if A$ = PAUL. The instructions on lines 40 and 50 will execute only if A$ is not equal to PAUL. Writing the program this way is awkward, but on the Sinclair, the TI, or any other computer that does not allow multi-statement lines, it is sometimes necessary. If you have a TI computer with TI Extended BASIC, you may write multi-statement lines, but you must separate the statements with two colons ("::").

IF-THEN statements open a whole world of possibilities to the imaginative programmer. Bear in mind that you are not restricted to testing whether one variable is precisely equal to another.

We can also check to see if the value of one variable is greater than the value of another, or less than the value of another, or simply not equal to the value of another.

For instance, we could say IF X < 1, which is read "If X is less than 1." The symbol "<" is called a "less-than" sign and tests to see if one value is less than another. Or we could say IF C > 500, which is read "If C is greater than 500." The symbol ">" is called a "greater-than" sign and tests to see if one value is greater than another. In the program that we just wrote we could have said IF A$ <> "PAUL". This is read as "If A$ is not equal to Paul." In this case, the conditions would only be true if A$ has been set equal to some string other than PAUL. The symbol "<>" means "is not equal to." Notice that it is made up of a less-than sign and a greater-than sign. Literally, it means "is lesser than or greater than," which is the same thing as saying "is not equal to." These symbols are called *relational operators* because they test the relationship between values in an IF-THEN statement.

We can even test more than one condition at a time. Consider this portion of a program statement: IF R < 1445 AND F$ = "FORD MUSTANG" and Z <> 2 THEN . . . . Notice the use of the word AND in this sentence. AND is called a *logical operator* because it tests for a logical relationship between the various conditions in the statement. In this case, the IF statement will be true only if the first condition AND the second condition AND the third condition are true.

On the other hand, we could say IF A$ = "SUSAN" OR A$ = "SUZIE" OR A$ = "SUE", which might have been useful in our name-checking program if the user had a large number of nicknames. OR is also a logical operator. This IF statement is true if the first condition OR the second condition OR the third condition is true, or if any combination of them should be true. Only if all three are false is this IF statement false.

Confused? Let's back up for a second and type this program:

Relational operators—Operators used to indicate a relation between two or more values, such as "greater than," "equal to," etc.

Logical operator—A word representing a logical operation.

```
10 PRINT "PLEASE TYPE A NUMBER"
20 INPUT N
30 IF N = −1 THEN END
40 IF N = 3 OR N = 22 OR N = 4555 THEN PRINT "THE
NUMBER YOU TYPED IS EITHER 3 OR 22 OR 4555"
50 IF N <> 14 AND N <> 200 THEN PRINT "THE NUMBER
YOU TYPED IS NEITHER 14 NOR 200"
60 IF N > 10 AND N < 150 THEN PRINT "THE NUMBER YOU
TYPED IS BETWEEN 10 AND 150"
70 IF N < 10 OR N > 150 THEN PRINT "THE NUMBER YOU
TYPED IS NOT BETWEEN 10 OR 150"
80 GOTO 10
```

This program is capable of making fairly complex decisions based on the numbers you type in response to the input prompt. Run it and try it with several different numbers; then examine its internal workings.

Line 40 tests to see if number N is any of three rather arbitrarily chosen numbers. To make this test, the program uses the OR operator. If one OR the other of these conditions is true, then the sentence is printed. Line 50 tests to see if the number is neither of two arbitrarily chosen numbers; it does this with the AND operator. If number N is not the first number AND if it is not the second number, then the sentence is printed.

Things get fancier with line 60, which tests to see if the number falls in the range between, but not including, 10 and 150. It does this by combining the AND operator with the greater-than and less-than operators. If number N is greater than 10 AND less than 150, the sentence is printed. Finally, line 70 tests to see if the number is not in this same range, by combining the greater-than and less-than operators with the OR operator. If the number is less than 10 OR greater than 150—and therefore definitely not in the range from 10 to 150—the sentence is printed. Notice that we did not use the AND operator in line 70. The computer would let us get away with it—try it and see—but it would make no sense. No number could be simultaneously greater than 150 and less than 10.

Under certain circumstances we can combine relational operators in a single condition test. The double symbol "< =", for instance, means "less-than-or-equal-to." On some computers it can also be written "$=<$". The symbol "$>=$" means "greater-than-or-equal-to." On some computers it can also be written "$=>$". We can use these symbols anywhere we would use any other relational operator. When we say IF A $<$ = 66 for example, the condition will be true when A is equal to 66 or when A is less than 66. By the opposite token, when we say IF A = $>$ 66, the condition will be true when A is equal to 66 or when A is greater than 66.

One of the most useful tricks in our most recent program is in line 30. This IF-THEN statement watches for our number to be equal to -1. When it is, the program terminates. The BASIC instruction END causes a program to stop executing and returns the computer to the immediate mode. This gives us a useful way of getting out of a program loop without having to hit the BREAK key. Programmers generally frown on programs that require the user to hit the BREAK key. While running this program, try typing -1 in response to the input prompt. You should be returned immediately to the command mode.

As a final review of the logical operators AND and OR, we might note that the computer uses these words in pretty much the same way that you do. When you say "I am going to the store if there is time and I have the money," you mean that both of these conditions must be true before you go to the store: You must have both the time AND the money. On the other hand, if you had said "I am going to the store if there is time or I have the money," you mean that only one of these conditions needs to be true, though it is okay if both are true: You must have the time OR the money (or both). And this is pretty much how the computer understands the words AND and OR.

The ability to test conditions, and have the computer make decisions based on these tests, is extremely valuable. Most of the programs in the remainder of this book will make use of this ability. There are computer scientists who believe that the decision-making properties of computers may one day allow these machines to "think" much as human beings do. Already, computers have been programmed to play games such as chess, which require fairly advanced decision-making capabilities, and these programs are based primarily on the principles that we have covered in this chapter.

Suggested Projects

1. Using at least one INPUT statement and several IF-THEN statements, write a program that asks the user a series of yes or no questions and reacts in an appropriate way to the user's response. For instance, the program could ask if the user is feeling well. If the user responds YES, the computer might say GLAD TO HEAR THAT. If the user responds NO, the computer might say THAT'S TOO BAD! If the user gives some response other than yes or no, the computer could reply I DON'T UNDERSTAND YOU.

2. Write a program that performs an arithmetic operation, or several arithmetic operations, on numbers input by the user while the program is running. (Hint: Perform the arithmetic operations on variables that have been previously assigned values with an INPUT statement. Remember to print a sentence that prompts the user for input.)

3. Write a program that not only performs arithmetic operations on numbers input by the user, but also asks the user what arithmetic operations to perform. (A possible solution to this problem is offered in the last chapter of this book. Hint: Your program will require INPUT and IF-THEN statements.)

4. Write a program that will echo words typed by the user—that is, print the words on the video display after the user has typed them—but will stop executing as soon as the user types STOP.

6
STORING DATA IN YOUR PROGRAM

Computers, as we saw in Chapter One, are for manipulating information, or *data*. Sometimes that information enters the computer from the outside world, perhaps via the INPUT statement. At other times, however, we will want to put large amounts of information right into our program. Suppose, for instance, that we wanted to write a program that would add fifteen numbers and give us a total. If we know in advance what the numbers will be, we can place them inside the program. But sometimes this can be an awkward process. We might write the program like this:

```
10 LET A = 10
20 LET B = 777
30 LET C = −45
40 LET D = 6.554
50 LET E = 55555
60 LET F = 65.4
70 LET G = 17
80 LET H = 542
90 LET I = 0.123
100 LET J = 666
110 LET K = 16443
120 LET L = −8234
130 LET M = 5
140 LET N = 32
```

Data—Information to be processed by a computer program.

```
150 LET O = 7677
160 PRINT A + B + C + D + E + F + G + H + I + J + K + L
+ M + N + O
```

This program would do the trick, all right, but it is overlong and rather tedious to write and uses a ridiculously large number of variables. There is, all in all, something clumsy and unpleasant about this program; it makes a person wonder if there might not be a better way to do this sort of thing.

Fortunately, there is: the DATA statement. The DATA statement is BASIC's way of allowing a programmer to insert large dollops of data into the middle of a program, with minimal effort and as little wasted space as possible. The above program, rewritten with a DATA statement, would look like this:

```
5 LET A = 0
10 READ X : LET A = A + X
20 IF X <> 5 THEN GOTO 10
30 PRINT A : END
40 DATA 10, 777, −45, 6.554, 55555, 65.4, 17, 542, 0.123, 666,
16443, −8234, 5, 32, 7677
```

Not only is this version a great deal neater than our earlier program, but it is considerably easier to write and takes up less space in your computer's memory. Computer memory can be a precious commodity, especially in the smaller computers like the Vic-20 and the Timex Sinclair 1000, though the Sinclair lacks the DATA instruction altogether— alas!—so that users of that computer would have to write this program using the first method.

How does the program work? The key is in the two words READ and DATA, which you will find in lines 10 and 40, respectively. The DATA instruction tells the computer that everything that follows, up until the end of the line or the next colon, is data, rather than further instructions. If the flow of a program passes through a line marked DATA, the computer will ignore it totally. In fact, we could have put our DATA line at the very beginning of the program without affecting the operation of the program in the least; however, it is a common programming practice to put DATA statements at the end of a program or near the end.

The computer continues ignoring the DATA statement until it encounters the instruction READ; then it begins paying close attention. The READ instruction, no matter where it appears in the program, tells the computer to find the first DATA statement in the program, take the first item of data from it—the computer can identify a single item of data because data items are separated by commas within the DATA statement—and assign the value of that item to the variable following the READ statement. In other words, the READ statement is a lot like the INPUT statement, except that it gets its data from a DATA statement rather than from the keyboard. The second time the computer encounters a READ statement in a program, it must fetch the second item of data from the DATA statement, or go to the next DATA statement if the first only held one item of data.

From then on, every time the computer encounters a READ statement it will proceed to take the next item of data from the DATA statements in the program until all the data is exhausted. If the program tries to read further data after all DATA statements have been exhausted, the computer will proclaim an OUT OF DATA error. (There is, however, a special instruction called RESTORE that causes the computer to return to the first DATA statement and begin the process over again.)

If this is less than clear, take a look at our program. When the computer encounters the READ statement in line 10, it immediately proceeds to the first DATA statement, which is in line 40, and fetches the first item of data from it—in this case, the number 10. It then sets the variable X equal to 10. The second portion of line 10—which TI BASIC users must type on a separate line—adds this value to the current value of variable A. The variable A was given a value of 0 in line 5. When we add 10 to A, its value becomes 10.

The computer then checks to see if X is not equal to 5, which happens to be the last item of data in our DATA statement. This protects the computer from attempting to read data that isn't there, which would cause an error condition. If X is indeed not equal to 5, it loops back to line 10 and reads another item of data. Since the second item in the DATA statement is 777, the computer now sets X equal to 777, and adds this to A, making A equal to 10 plus 777, or 787.

The computer checks again to see if X is equal to 5; since it is not, the computer reads yet another item of data—this time, −45—sets X equal to it, and adds X to A. This loop continues, with the computer reading every item of data until it comes to 5, the last item of data; this automatically terminates the loop. Otherwise, the computer would continue looking for data that is not there, and an error would result. By this time, however, every number in the DATA statement has been added to A; thus, A represents the total of all the numbers. This value is then printed on the screen, and the program comes to an end.

If you'll look back at the previous program, you'll see that both programs produce the same results, but that the second version does its job in a much more elegant manner. With the DATA statement, there is no need to use a large number of variables or to set each one equal to a specific number in a separate assignment statement. Instead, the DATA statement holds the numbers in an organized manner until they are needed, at which point they are parceled out one by one in the READ loop.

We can also store strings in a DATA statement, which can prove useful if, for instance, we wish to print a list on the computer's screen, as in this program:

```
10 READ A$
20 IF A$ = "END" THEN END
30 PRINT A$
40 GOTO 10
50 DATA CHARLEY HANCOCK, GRETA ABELSON, LARRY
DOMINICO, JANE HOROWITZ, GEORGE SIMON, LARA
JONES, JIM SUTTON, FRANCES JOHNSON, END
```

If you run this program, you'll find that its output looks like this:

```
CHARLEY HANCOCK
GRETA ABELSON
LARRY DOMINICO
JANE HOROWITZ
GEORGE SIMON
LARA JONES
JIM SUTTON
FRANCES JOHNSON
```

The beauty of this program is that we can extend our list indefinitely, by adding to the program more and more DATA statements containing more and more names, as long as we make sure that the last data item is the string END, which terminates the program.

There are many tricks that we can play with such a program. Suppose, for instance, that we wanted to print the names on the screen in two columns instead of one. We could change lines 10 through 30 as follows:

```
10 READ A$, B$
20 IF B$ = "END" THEN END
30 PRINT A$, B$
```

On most computers, the output of this program should look something like this:

CHARLEY HANCOCK	GRETA ABELSON
LARRY DOMINICO	JANE HOROWITZ
GEORGE SIMON	LARA JONES
JIM SUTTON	FRANCES JOHNSON

Line 10 now reads the values of two items of data into two variables; to make a READ statement read more than one variable, the variables need only be separated by commas. The computer then prints them on the screen in a neat two-column format. Note that when we use the PRINT statement to display the two strings, the variables following the PRINT instruction are separated from one another by a comma. This comma tells the computer to move forward by a single *tab location* before it prints the second variable. What—and where—is a tab location? Many computers, such as the TRS-80 Models I and III, have four tab locations on their screens. The first is located on the left-hand edge of the screen, the second is one-fourth of the way across the screen, the third halfway across the screen, and

Tab location—The location on the computer screen at which the next character in a PRINT statement will be displayed if it is preceded by an unquoted tab symbol (which is usually a comma).

the fourth three-quarters of the way across. Other computers, such as the VIC-20, have only two tab locations, one on the left-hand edge and the other halfway across. These locations are invisible to your eye, but the computer always remembers where they are. When the computer encounters a comma in a PRINT statement, it automatically spaces to the next tab location—or to the beginning of the next line if it has already gone past the last tab location on the current line—and resumes printing at that location. You can look at the comma as being a command in the BASIC language, just as PRINT and GOTO are commands. The comma, in effect, means TAB FORWARD. Remember, however, that the comma means this only when it appears between items in a PRINT statement. Commas may also be used in other BASIC statements, such as DATA statements and READ statements, with other meanings altogether. Nonetheless, comma tabs are a nice way to print neatly formatted columns of data on the computer's screen.

As the two columns are being printed, line 20 maintains its vigilant lookout for the END marker, but it now becomes important that the END marker is read into variable B$. If it should be read by variable A$, we will receive an OUT OF DATA ERROR when the computer attempts to read nonexistent data into B$.

You'll also notice that the two columns of names fall neatly into two groups: male and female. This is a result of the way the data items are organized within the DATA statement. We have done this for no particular reason, except to indicate that the organization of data items within a DATA statement can be matched to screen format in such a way that separate and distinct groups of data can be printed on the screen in separate and distinct fashion. The names might be printed out in groupings according to which classroom or scout troop or hobby club the person belongs to, for instance.

There is no reason to restrict the data in our DATA statement to either string or numeric data; we can use both at the same time, as long as we are careful about matching the proper type of variable with the proper type of data item. Consider the following variation on our last program:

```
10 READ A$, A
20 IF A$ = "END" THEN END
```

```
30 PRINT A$, A
40 GOTO 10
50 DATA JACK JACOBOWITZ, 85, LYNN FRELS, 79, PETE
SMITH, 56, LINDA NEE, 99, JOAN SCOTT, 90, END, 0
```

The output of this program would look like this:

JACK JACOBOWITZ	85
LYNN FRELS	79
PETE SMITH	56
LINDA NEE	99
JOAN SCOTT	90

By alternating string and numeric data, we are able to pair the names with numbers. Perhaps the numbers represent the scores these individuals made on a test, the numbers on their athletic jerseys, or their times for finishing a race. To vary this program, change the comma after the A$ in line 30 to a semicolon (";"). This tells the computer to suspend the tab and print the number directly after the name, like this:

JACK JACOBOWITZ 85

The semicolon comes in handy in a number of situations, of course. As we noted before, the computer automatically registers a carriage return after it executes a PRINT statement—that is, when one PRINT statement follows another, the second statement automatically prints on the next line rather than farther along on the first. Try this example, in case you are having trouble envisioning what we mean:

```
10 PRINT "HELLO"
20 PRINT "GOOD-BYE"
```

The output of the program looks like this:

```
HELLO
GOOD-BYE
```

Although we did not tell the computer to do so, it moved down a line after printing the first statement to print the second. Unless we tell it explicitly to do otherwise, it will always do this. The way we tell the computer not to execute a carriage return after performing a PRINT is with a semicolon. To see what we mean, change the first line of our two-line program to this:

10 PRINT "HELLO";

The output of the program now looks like this:

HELLOGOOD-BYE

You'll notice that the computer fails to put a space between the two strings; the semicolon tells it to begin printing the second string *immediately* after the first. You might also have noticed that it did not do this when we printed the number after the name in the previous program. This is because most computers automatically put a space in front of a number when it is printed on the display, which allows neat formatting of numbers. Of course, if we don't want a space in front of the number . . . .

To format our string more neatly, we might change line 10 once again:

10 PRINT "HELLO   "

Now there is a space after the first string, which changes the output to this:

HELLO GOOD-BYE

Most versions of BASIC contain a good number of tricks for printing numbers and strings on the computer's screen. Some even allow you to specify the exact position on the screen where you want the next item to be printed. The Apple computer, for instance, has a pair of commands called HTAB and VTAB, which stand for "horizontal tab" and "vertical tab," respectively. With these commands, we can move the computer's "PRINT position" by a specified number of spaces vertically and horizontally and thus control the specific location at which the next PRINT statement will be executed. The TRS-80 Models I and III have a command called PRINT@ (pronounced "print at"), which allows the programmer to name the specific numbered location on the screen where the next item will be printed. Unfortunately, because these sorts of commands differ widely from computer to computer, and because many computers have no such commands at all, we will not be able to go into any detail here about how they work.

We have wandered far afield from our main subject, however, which was the storage of data in programs. Actually, this is all we have to say about it at the moment, though we will return to it later in this book. For the moment, however, we are going to return to the subject of loops, which, next to variables and IF-THEN statements, are among the most important techniques the programmer has at his or her disposal.

Suggested Projects

1. Write a program with a DATA statement containing the names of every member of your family, followed by their nicknames or the names they like to be called by. Have the computer print this information on the screen in two columns, one column containing the formal names and the second the corresponding nicknames.

2. Find out how many tab positions there are on your computer's screen. Write a program that will fill each tab position with a number, perhaps the same number repeated over and over, forming multiple columns on the screen. Hint: You will need to place your PRINT statement in a program loop—and don't forget to use a comma.

7

LOOPING

We saw in an earlier chapter how easy it is to make a program go in loops, that is, execute the same series of instructions over and over again. We simply add a GOTO statement at the end of the segment that we want the computer to repeat, so that the computer continually jumps back to the beginning of the loop. We have seen that it is fairly easy to make the computer jump out of a loop without forcing the user to hit the BREAK key: Merely slip an IF-THEN statement in at a judiciously chosen location, so that execution of the loop will terminate at a desirable moment—when we input a prearranged number, for instance, or when we read a certain item from a DATA statement. With the clever application of a few more IF-THEN statements, we can even arrange it so that the loop will behave differently each time the program executes, as in our program in which the computer made appropriate responses depending on the name that you entered at the input prompt.

Here is a little secret that every BASIC programmer should know:

It is possible to achieve all of the effects just described with a single BASIC program statement. We call this statement—actually a matched pair of statements—a FOR-NEXT loop. It allows us to create a loop, define its limits, break out of it at a desired moment, and even vary its behavior every time it executes—without using any GOTO or IF-THEN statements, although we can use such things within the loop if we desire.

How does it work? As usual, we'll explain with a demonstration. Type this program:

```
10 FOR X = 1 TO 1000
20 PRINT X
30 NEXT X
40 PRINT "FINISHED!"
```

And run it. Whoops—the computer's gone crazy again, typing numbers all down the screen with no sign of a letup. Don't reach for the BREAK key, however; be patient, and the computer will come back to its senses. There; it's stopped. What exactly happened?

Well, notice that the numbers the computer printed are sequential, that is, it counted in an orderly fashion from 1 to 1000, ending something like this:

```
992
993
994
995
996
997
998
999
1000
FINISHED!
```

Now look back again at the program. The first line reads FOR X = 1 TO 1000. That would seem to explain the fact that it counted consecutively from one to one thousand; the words 1 TO 1000 appear right in the program. What does FOR X mean? It tells the computer to set X equal to all the numbers between and including 1 and 1000, one after another, using a new value each time the computer goes through the loop. The first time the computer encounters this statement it sets X equal to the first number in the specified sequence, which in this case is 1—just as though we had written LET X = 1. The computer then passes on to line 20. What happened to all the other numbers it was supposed to set X equal to? We're coming to that.

Line 20 tells the computer to print the value of X on the display. X is now equal to 1, so the computer prints a 1. Line 30 reads, simply, NEXT X. This statement has a rather odd effect. It forces the computer to remember where it last executed a FOR statement, like the one in line 10, and makes it jump back to that point in the program, as though it had encountered a GOTO.

When the computer jumps back to the FOR statement, it checks to make sure that the variable in that statement—in this case, the variable X—is the same as in the NEXT statement. If not, it prints an error message.

Most Microsoft versions of BASIC—see the list of computers using Microsoft BASIC in the first chapter—will allow you to drop the variable after the word NEXT, since it is not absolutely necessary to the operation of the loop. Non-Microsoft BASICS, such as those in Atari, Timex Sinclair, and TI computers, usually require it. We will continue including it in this book, because your computer might insist on it and because it makes the programs somewhat easier to understand.

The computer then looks at the sequence of numbers specified in the FOR statement—in this case, 1 TO 1000. It adds 1 to the value of the variable; if that doesn't take it beyond the end of the specified sequence, it then proceeds to the next statement in the program. In this case, the computer adds 1 to the variable X, making X equal to $1 + 1$, or 2. Since this doesn't make X larger than the end of the sequence, it continues on to the next statement.

When the computer is called upon to print the value of X in the next statement, it will print a 2. And when it next encounters the NEXT statement in line 30, it will return to line 10 and set X equal to the next number in the sequence, which is 3. Then in line 20 it will print 3 on the screen and in line 30 it will be ordered to return to line 10, and so on.

If we follow this loop through to its logical conclusion, we will see that eventually the computer will set X equal to 1000. After printing 1000 on the screen and being forced back to line 10 by the NEXT statement, it will proceed to set X equal to 1001. However, this time it will notice that it has exceeded the limits of the specified sequence. Instead of printing 1001 on the screen, the computer skips over every statement in the program until it comes to the word NEXT and executes the statement immediately following the NEXT statement. Program flow will continue onward from that point. On most computers, if we were to place a PRINT X statement after the end of the loop, however, we would discover that the value of X at that point is now 1001—even though this value was not printed while the loop was executing. This is important to remember, should you plan to further manipulate the value of X after the loop is over.

It shouldn't be difficult to see the usefulness of a FOR-NEXT loop. It allows us to set the beginning and end of a loop, the number of times that it will execute before carrying on with the rest of the program, or ending, and even what the value of our chosen variable—in this case, X—will be each time through the loop. Of course, we don't necessarily have to do anything with the value of the variable; it can simply be used for counting the number of times through the loop.

One important use of such a loop is simply to slow things down. Sometimes programs execute a little faster than we'd like them to, and we want to delay them for a moment. A loop that causes such a delay in a program is called, amazingly enough, a *delay loop*.

Suppose, for instance, that we want to give our program a title sequence, like a movie. Perhaps we want the titles to appear one after another, slowly enough for the user to read them. We might do it something like this:

```
10 PRINT : PRINT: PRINT : PRINT "THE AMAZING, DO-
EVERYTHING PROGRAM!"
20 FOR X = 1 TO 1000 : NEXT X
30 PRINT : PRINT "BY JOE DOAKS"
40 FOR X = 1 TO 1000 : NEXT X
50 PRINT: PRINT "WITH A CAST OF THOUSANDS!"
60 FOR X = 1 TO 1000 : NEXT X
70 PRINT : PRINT "THE END"
```

The loops on lines 20, 40, and 60 really don't do anything except waste time. In effect, the computer stops and counts to a thousand, so that there will be a delay between the printing of each line of the credit sequence. If you run the program, however, you may be surprised at how short the delay actually is. Computers count very quickly.

Delay loop—A program loop designed simply to slow down execution of a program.

Another use of a FOR-NEXT loop involves DATA statements. If we know how many items are in each data statement, we can easily set up a FOR-NEXT loop to the data items, instead of the more rudimentary loop that we used in the programs in the previous chapter. Of course, the loop that we used offers us the advantage of being able to rewrite the DATA statements without having to rewrite the loop. As long as the last item in the DATA statement read END, it didn't matter how many data items there were. On the other hand, with a FOR-NEXT loop we must specify within the loop itself the number of times that the loop is going to execute.

There are a number of possible variations on the FOR-NEXT loop that you should be aware of. For instance, it is not necessary to start the loop at 1. We could as easily say FOR X = 1000 TO 5006 or FOR I = 34 TO 69. Furthermore, we don't have to count through the loop by ones. If we want to count through the loop two units, or "steps," at a time, we must add a STEP clause to the FOR statement, like this:

```
10 FOR X = 2 TO 100 STEP 2
20 PRINT X
30 NEXT X
```

This loop will count from 2 to 100 by twos: 2, 4, 6, 8, 10, 12, and so forth. Try it and see.

You can use any number that you want for the STEP number—within reasonable limits. Your computer might refuse to accept a STEP number larger than, say, 65,000 or so. We can even count through a loop backward, using a negative STEP number. Change line 10 of the preceding program to FOR X = 100 TO 2 STEP −2 and see what happens.

Intelligent use of FOR-NEXT loops can make the programmer's task much easier and can reduce the amount of computer memory required to create a loop. Such frugal use of memory is particularly important in very small computers, where complex programs must be written with constant attention to the careful use of storage space. A computer with only 2K of memory, such as the Timex Sinclair, can hold only a relatively small BASIC program.

Incidentally, the "K" in 2K of memory is a measurement of computer memory space. It is short for *kilobyte,* or 1,024 bytes. A *byte* is the amount of memory required for the storage of a single character, such as the letter "A" or the number "1" or any other character in the computer's character set. It is an oddity of most computers, by the way, that they store BASIC commands in their memories as single characters. The command PRINT, for instance, or GOTO, is stored as a single character, like a letter of the alphabet. This memory storage technique is called *compression* and allows you to fit larger BASIC programs into smaller amounts of memory. If you have limited memory in your computer and need to structure your programs accordingly, you might recall that BASIC commands take up less storage space than strings of the same length.

Kilobyte—1,024 bytes; usually abbreviated as "K."

Byte—A unit of computer memory; the amount of memory required to store a single alphanumeric character.

Compression—The process by which key words in a program are reduced to a single byte.

Suggested Projects

1. Write a loop that will print out every fourth number between 56 and 911. Then rewrite it to print through the same list backward.

2. Write a delay loop that will cause a program to pause for exactly ten seconds. Time the loop with the second hand of a watch. Experiment until you find exactly how many times you must loop in order to delay for ten seconds. (Some computers contain a built-in clock and can be made to print the current time—or the time elapsed since the power was turned on—with a single BASIC command. Check your manual to see if the computer you are using has such a clock. If so, you can make the loop time itself, instead of relying on a watch. In fact, you might try writing a program that will use an IF-THEN statement combined with the computer's internal clock to delay for exactly ten seconds.)

3. Write a program that reads the contents of a DATA statement using a FOR-NEXT loop rather than the GOTO loops used in the last chapter.

8
GETTING
THE
PICTURE

One subject we haven't touched on yet in this book is *graphics,* which is the creation of pictures on the computer's video display. There is a reason for this. When the BASIC language was developed, in the mid-1960s, computers with video displays were relatively rare. Most computer terminals used printers rather than television screens. These printers produced so-called "hard copy" of the user's transactions with the computer—that is, everything typed by the computer or the user was printed on long sheets of paper. This explains why BASIC uses the word PRINT for displaying messages on the video screen; the command was originally intended to put messages on a printer. Today, some versions of BASIC use the command LPRINT (for "line print") to send messages to the printer.

There was little need, in those early days of the BASIC language, to include commands for drawing pictures. Who needed to draw pictures on a printer? You could hardly use a printer for playing video games.

Things have changed, of course. Modern home computers almost invariably come with their own video displays or with equipment for hooking them up to ordinary home television sets. Graphics have become an important element of computing—and not just in video games. Businesses, for instance, use the computer's graphic capabilities to draw charts and graphs. Scientists can simulate physical

---

Graphics—Pictorial images, especially those produced by a computer.

processes visually on the computer's display. Filmmakers can use computers to create dazzling visual effects, such as those in the movie *Tron*.

Most modern versions of BASIC contain commands for creating graphics; these commands were added by later programmers, who saw a need that was not envisioned by the creators of BASIC. Because these commands were not included in the original BASIC, they vary wildly from one computer to the next. A graphics command on the TI-99/4A, for instance, may not bear the slightest resemblance to a graphics command on the Radio Shack Color Computer.

This is not entirely the fault of the programmers who wrote these versions of BASIC. Graphics commands in any computer language are extremely hardware-dependent. This means that the language can only allow you to do what the hardware of the computer allows it to do. Different computers have different graphics capabilities, and this is largely the result of hardware, not software, although several popular computers have powerful graphics capabilities in their hardware that are not taken advantage of by their built-in programming language. The Commodore 64 is a prime example of this. A few computers are incapable of producing graphics at all. Others can produce graphics only in black-and-white, while still others are capable of creating pictures in brilliant color. Computers like the Timex Sinclair 1000 and the TRS-80 Models I and III feature only *low-resolution graphics,* with little detail, while computers like the Apple, the Atari, the Coleco Adam, the IBM Personal Computer, the Timex Sinclair 2068, the Spectravideo, the Radio Shack Color Computer, the VIC-20, the Commodore 64, and the TI-99/4A can create vivid, *high-resolution* graphics. A few computers, such as the Atari, the Coleco Adam, the Spectravideo, the TI-99/4A, and the Commodore 64, allow the programmer to design special

---

Low-resolution graphics—Computer images constructed from blocky graphics characters.

High-resolution graphics—Computer images containing fine detail.

graphics images called *sprites,* which can easily be moved and animated. The moving figures in most coin-operated arcade games are sprites.

Thus, we can do little in this book to teach you the specifics of programming graphics on the computer you are using. For that, you must consult your manual, which will probably devote a section to the subject. (There will almost certainly be other books on the market as well, discussing graphics for your particular computer.) However, even though we can't go into it in great detail, this chapter will touch on some of the essential principles of graphics programming, which will remain pretty much the same from computer to computer.

The simplest graphics command that any computer can feature is one that will clear the screen—erase the current image on the video display and leave a blank screen behind. This allows the programmer to build a graphics display from scratch, without having to worry about leftover pieces of text or earlier graphics. Alas, the command that performs this task is quite unstandardized, even among computers that use Microsoft BASIC. On the TRS-80s, the IBM Personal Computer, and the Sinclairs it is CLS, short for CLear Screen; on the Apple it is HOME, because, in addition to clearing the screen, it moves the cursor to its "home" position—at the upper left-hand corner of the screen; on the Atari it is PRINT CHR$(125); on Commodore computers, such as the VIC-20 and Commodore 64, it is PRINT CHR$(147); on the TI-99/4A it is CALL CLEAR. Some computers also feature a key on the keyboard that the programmer can use to clear the screen "manually" whenever it is becoming a bit cluttered. This key is usually marked CLEAR or CLR. However, this can only be used when no program is actually running on the computer.

Once you've cleared the screen, you can begin drawing on it. The simplest way to produce graphics is with the PRINT statement. The following program, for instance, will draw a simple face on your computer's screen:

Sprites—Special graphics images, available on some computers, that can be easily animated and moved about the video display.

```
 10 PRINT  "          *        *              "
 20 PRINT  "      *                *          "
 30 PRINT  "      *                  *        "
 40 PRINT  "                                  "
 50 PRINT  "   *       *         *        *   "
 60 PRINT  "                                  "
 70 PRINT  "   *             *           *    "
 80 PRINT  "                                  "
 90 PRINT  "       *    *    *   *   *      * "
100 PRINT  "         *              *         "
110 PRINT  "            *        *            "
```

Though effective enough in its way, this sort of graphics presentation probably won't impress your friends with your abilities as a programmer. However, this does not mean that we have to abandon the PRINT statement as a method of producing graphics in BASIC. Most computers feature a special set of graphics characters that can be printed on the video display just as you would print ordinary characters— letters, numbers, and so on. These graphics characters look rather like tiny pieces from a jigsaw puzzle; and just as the pieces of a jigsaw puzzle can be put together to form a pic- ture, so these graphics characters can be pieced together into an image of the programmer's own design. Graphics characters are usually assigned numbers and can be printed with the CHR$ (from *cha*racter) function. This function can be used to print any character that the computer ordinarily accepts as part of a string. To print the letter A, for example, we would type PRINT CHR$(65), since 65 is the code number usually assigned by the computer to the letter A. (The com- puter assigns such code numbers to all characters.) Though this is a somewhat roundabout way of printing letters, it also works with graphics characters. To print the graphics character assigned the number 175, for instance, you would type PRINT CHR$(175). The computer would then display graphics character 175 on the computer's screen. Most computers even allow us to concatenate graphics characters together into a string and assign the result to a string vari- able, like this:

```
LET A$ = CHR$(175) + CHR$(160) + CHR$(131) +
CHR$(128) + CHR$(191)
```

In this way, we can effectively set a string variable equal to a picture. Then, when we print that string variable on the screen—PRINT A$, in this example—the computer will display the graphics image that we have designed.

To find out what numbers your computer assigns to what graphics characters, consult the manual. Most computer handbooks contain a table of graphics characters, with pictures of the characters followed by their assigned numbers. Some computers, such as the Timex Sinclair and the VIC-20, even have the graphics characters displayed on the keyboard, so that graphic images can be typed directly into a program, usually by striking the key with the graphics image on it simultaneously with a special control key. The VIC-20 keyboard, for instance, produces graphics characters when the appropriate key is struck along with the SHIFT key or the key with the Commodore logo printed on it. The Sinclair produces graphics characters after the special GRAPHICS key has been pressed, putting the computer into graphics mode. Other computers, such as the Atari, allow graphics to be produced from the keyboard but do not print the graphics characters on the keyboard itself, relying on the programmer to find out which key represents which character by reading the manual.

The graphics that we create with graphics characters are low-resolution graphics; they are usually rather blocky-looking and lacking in detail. Many computers also have the ability to produce the more detailed, high-resolution graphics. To produce high-resolution graphics, we must control individual *pixels* on the computer's video display.

What is a pixel? The term is short for "pictorial element." The building blocks of graphics images, pixels are the smallest details that we can produce in a computer-generated picture. A pixel will appear as a single point of light on the computer's screen, the smallest portion of any image that we can produce on the display. Many versions of BASIC offer a command that allows the programmer to turn on a pixel of his or her choice—that is, to make that pixel become visible and even to determine its color. On

Pixel—The smallest unit of a graphics image.

most computers, this command is PLOT. Some computers also offer a command for turning pixels off—that is, for making them invisible. This command is usually UNPLOT. The low-resolution TRS-80 offers programmers a sort of pseudo–high-resolution pixel control with the commands SET and RESET, which do the job of the PLOT and UNPLOT commands but with chunky, low-resolution pixels. The Timex Sinclair 1000 uses PLOT and UNPLOT similarly.

Generally, the PLOT command must be followed by a set of numbers indicating the location of the pixel on the screen and the color in which it is to be displayed, assuming the computer has color capability. The pixel is usually identified by its coordinates on the screen. PLOT 10, 27, 3, for instance, might tell the computer to turn on the pixel that is ten pixel positions from the left side of the screen and twenty-seven pixel positions from the top of the screen and to display that pixel in color number 3. The specific use of the PLOT command will vary from computer to computer.

On many computers, the programmer must announce in a program that he or she wishes to work in the high-resolution graphics mode before a pixel can be plotted. On the Apple, the command that activates the high-resolution mode is HGR. The Atari has several different high-resolution modes, depending on the degree of resolution and number of colors desired. The specific graphics mode must be identified by typing the appropriate number after the command GRAPHICS.

High-resolution graphics are a tricky business on most computers and can be mastered only with a great deal of practice. A modicum of artistic talent is helpful, too, though not absolutely necessary. Many recent computers offer an interesting alternative to high-resolution graphics: *redefinable graphics characters*. These computers, which

---

Redefinable graphics characters—A special process, available on some computers, by which characters that can be displayed on the computer's screen—including letters of the alphabet, numbers, and standard graphics characters—can be changed into miniature pictorial images of the user's design. These miniature images can then be used to construct larger graphics images.

include the Atari, the VIC-20, the Commodore 64, the Coleco Adam, the IBM Personal Computer, the TI-99/4 and 99/4A, the Spectravideo, and the Timex Sinclair 2068, allow you to design your own special graphics characters, from which you may build graphic images. Although this may not give you the ability to plot the pixel of your choice anywhere on the screen, it does allow you to turn on individual pixels within the custom graphics characters—and thus design your own personalized set of graphics characters. These characters can then be used like the pieces of the previously mentioned jigsaw puzzle to build highly effective pictorial images, except that this time you are allowed to design the pieces of the jigsaw puzzle yourself, instead of using those prepared for you by the computer manufacturer.

Alas, on most computers these redefinable characters are even harder to use than the standard high-resolution graphics modes. A notable exception to this is the TI-99/4A, which offers the programmer a very simple command (CALL CHAR) for designing special graphics characters and using them in programs.

A few computers make an extra effort to ease the programmer's entrance into computer graphics design. Many, such as the Apple, the Atari, the Radio Shack Color Computer, the Timex Sinclair 2000, and the IBM Personal Computer, offer commands for drawing lines between specified points on the screen. The Color Computer, the IBM, and the Sinclair 2068 also feature commands, such as CIR-CLE, that allow you to draw curves and shapes tailored to your specifications. The Apple uses a special system called *shape tables,* that allows instructions for creating graphics images to be stored in the computer's memory and executed with the DRAW command. TI-99/4A Extended BASIC allows the programmer to design, and even animate, special characters and "sprites" with simple commands (such as CALL SPRITE).

Shape table—A graphics system used on the Apple computers with which instructions for building a graphics image may be stored in the computer's memory, then executed with a single BASIC command.

At the opposite extreme, a few computers, such as the Commodore VIC-20 and the Commodore 64, offer virtually no graphics commands at all, other than the simple ability to specify in which color the screen characters are to be printed. Oddly, this doesn't mean that the programmer cannot perform fancy graphics tricks on these machines; it is just a great deal harder, perhaps beyond the abilities of the novice programmer. The VIC-20, for instance, is capable of high-resolution graphics, even though there are no commands in VIC BASIC to support this capability. Fortunately, there are often special programs available, from the computer's manufacturer or from companies that specialize in programs for that computer, that will help the programmer achieve spectacular graphics effects with a minimum of effort.

Graphics programming can be one of the most satisfying projects that the microcomputer programmer can engage in. Though graphics-oriented programs are generally not easy to write, the result is often worth the effort.

Suggested Projects

1. Write a short program that prints the word HEL-LO on an otherwise completely blank screen.

2. Using PRINT statements and asterisks, can you write a program that will draw, on the computer's screen, a simple picture of a man or a woman? How about a picture of a cat? A giraffe? A square with a star inside?

3. Consult your computer's manual to find the proper BASIC instruction for turning on a single pixel on your computer's screen. (The instruction will probably be either PLOT or SET, though if you are using a TI or a Commodore computer, it is possible that no such command exists.) Experiment with this command, learning to turn on pixels at any point on the video display. Now see if you can write a short program that will use this command to draw a horizontal, and then a vertical, line across the computer's screen. If you are successful, see if you can figure out how to draw a diagonal line. (Hint: You might want to employ a FOR-NEXT loop in this program, though it is not absolutely necessary.)

4. Once you have written a program to draw a line on the computer's screen, see if you can write a program that will move a dot from one side of the

screen to the other. (Hint: This program will be almost exactly like the program that draws a line on the screen, with the addition of one extra step. Can you figure out what that extra step should be? Remember that the line you drew was made up of a series of dots, one immediately after the other.)

5. If your computer is capable of producing color graphics, find out what command is used to change the background color of the screen. See if you can write a short program that uses a FOR-NEXT loop to display all of the possible background colors, one after another. Also, see if it is possible to control the color of characters on the computer's screen. Write a program that will display all possible character colors.

9

THE FINAL PROGRAM

At this point, you know enough about the BASIC language to produce some useful programs. What sort of programs you produce is up to you, of course. They can be playful or serious in intent, carefully designed or wildly experimental, intended for a specific purpose or just to show off your newfound skills.

To point you in the right direction, this final chapter will offer a single program, which we will study in considerable detail, making changes and improvements as we see fit.

The program looks like this:

```
5 REM CALCULATOR PROGRAM
10 PRINT "NUMBER";:  INPUT N1
20 PRINT "OPERATION";:   INPUT OP$
30 PRINT "NUMBER";:   INPUT N2
40 IF OP$ = "+" THEN GOTO 100
50 IF OP$ = "−" THEN GOTO 200
60 IF OP$ = "/" THEN GOTO 300
70 IF OP$ = "*" THEN GOTO 400
80 IF OP$ = "C" THEN GOTO 10
90 GOTO 20
100 LET R = N1 + N2 : GOTO 500
200 LET R = N1 − N2 : GOTO 500
300 LET R = N1 / N2 : GOTO 500
400 LET R = N1 * N2
500 PRINT "RESULT =    " ;R
510 LET N1 = R
520 GOTO 20
```

This is a simple program to simulate the operation of an electronic calculator, something your computer can do exceedingly well. It allows the user to type in numbers and arithmetic operators in response to the input prompt. When you run the program, it will print the question NUMBER? on the display. You may then type in a number and press RETURN. Then the computer prints OPERATION? You may respond to this prompt with one of four possible operators: +, −, *, or /, for addition, subtraction, multiplication, and division, respectively. The prompt will return, asking you for a second number; when you input another number, the computer will perform the requested operation on the first and second numbers and print the result on the screen. Suppose, for instance, that your first number is 3, the operation is +, and the second number is 6. The result will be 9, which is 3 plus 6. Notice that this program operates in exactly the same fashion as an electronic calculator: You give it a number, just as you press the number keys on a calculator; tell it what operation you want, just as you press the plus, minus, multiplication, or division keys on a calculator; and then give it a second number. It, in turn, gives you a result.

The computer then offers you a chance to perform further operations on the result, just as a pocket calculator would. If you now respond * to the OPERATION? prompt, and 3 to the NUMBER? prompt, the computer will print a result of 27, which is 9 multiplied by 3. And so forth. You may continue performing operations on the results of previous operations as long as you'd like, just as though you were using a pocket calculator. If at any time you want to start again, type the letter C (for CLEAR) in response to the OPERATOR? prompt. The result value will be cleared to 0, and the first NUMBER? prompt will return.

How does the program work? Let's examine it line by line. The first line contains a BASIC command we have not seen before in this book: REM. REM is short for "remark." It simply tells the computer to ignore everything following it on that program line and pass on to the next line. This allows the programmer to inject comments into the body of the program, to aid in future examination of the program, to aid others who may need to understand it, or even just to identify the program for future reference, in case it gets laid away in a drawer and forgotten. Although in this example we have used the REM statement simply to add a title to the program, you may include such statements at any point in a program. Remember, however, that everything—everything!—that follows such a statement on a program line will be ignored; thus, all REM statements should be placed either at the end of the multi-statement lines or on lines by themselves. REM statements are recommended for most programs, because they make it easier for the programmer, and others, to return to the program at a later date to make revisions; otherwise, without extensive remarks, even the person who wrote the program might find it totally incomprehensible. Of course, if the memory in your computer is limited, you might not have space for very many remarks, especially in longer programs, in which case they can be omitted without harm to the program.

Line 10 prints the NUMBER? prompt on the screen, accepts numerical input from the keyboard, and sets variable N1 equal to that input. Line 20 prints the OPERATION? prompt on the screen, accepts string input from the keyboard, and sets variable OP$ equal to that input. Line 30 behaves exactly like line 10, except that it uses the variable N2. Lines 40 through 80 examine the operator name contained in variable OP$ and "branch" to the appropriate routine to perform the arithmetic. If the computer does not recognize OP$, line 90 returns it to the OPERATOR? prompt, to get a valid operator symbol to replace the unrecognized one. Lines 100 through 400 perform the addition, subtraction, multiplication, and division operations on the values of variables N1 and N2, depending on which operation was requested. When the appropriate operation has been performed, these lines branch to the instructions on line 500, which prints the result; line 510, which sets variable N1 equal to it, and line 520, which branches back to the operator prompt. In this way, the results of previous operations are allowed to "ride" in variable N1, with the new numbers being input into variable N2. If the C option is requested, the computer returns to line 10, which receives a new value for variable N1, starting the process all over again.

There are a couple of things you might want to notice about this program. The first is the variable names. Notice how they have been chosen so that they sound at least a little like the values they represent. The two numbers, for instance, are contained in N1 and N2—for Number 1 and Number 2. The operation is contained in OP$.

Notice also how the program checks to make sure you gave it a valid operator in response to the OPERATOR? prompt. Lines 40 through 80 check for every possible operator and branch to the appropriate routines, but if the value of OP$ doesn't match any of these operators, the program "falls through" to line 90, which branches back to the OPERATOR? prompt. Line 90 is very important to this program. The computer will make it all the way to line 90 only when the operator input by the user is not one of the operators that the program accepts. It is tempting for a programmer to assume that all input from a user will be valid—that is, that the user will never type input that the program cannot use. Alas, this is not always the case. Sometimes the user will make a typographical error, or perhaps misunderstand the purpose of a program and type something that the computer doesn't understand. Line 90 is a way of catching this sort of input. Without line 90, improper input would cause the computer to perform in a very odd manner. Writing a program in such a way that it will catch invalid input from the user is called "idiot proofing," a term that may be unfair to well-intentioned users who do occasionally make mistakes but that nonetheless catches the flavor of the careful programmer's task. You must be sure to think of everything that could go wrong when a program is executing and take it into account within the program. Make sure that no "idiot," by giving improper input, can make your program behave in a way it was not intended to. We will consider several other ways of idiot-proofing this program before we are finished.

For instance, we might add a line or two to print instructions for the user, since we are expecting them to be able to use this program without training and with only a series of prompts for guidance. The instructions might be something along the lines of PLEASE TYPE NUMBERS IN RESPONSE TO THE 'NUMBER?' PROMPT. IN RESPONSE TO THE 'OPERATOR?' PROMPT, PLEASE TYPE ONE OF THE FOLLOWING SYMBOLS: '+', '−', '*', OR '/', DEPENDING ON WHETHER YOU ARE INTERESTED IN PERFORMING ADDI-

TION, SUBTRACTION, MULTIPLICATION, OR DIVISION. PRESS 'C' TO CLEAR THE RESULTS OF PREVIOUS OPERATIONS. The instructions can be a great deal more detailed than this, of course; that's up to you. Note, by the way, that these instructions use apostrophes instead of quote marks to indicate quoted phrases. This is because genuine quotation marks would confuse the computer as to what was string data and what was not. In computerese, the apostrophe is often referred to as the "single quote" and the regular quotation mark as the "double quote."

We might also add to the routine that checks the validity of the input, to make it respond more quickly than it does in this version. As it is now written, the program doesn't check to see if the operator is correct until after the second number is typed, which could be exceedingly confusing—and frustrating—for the user when an incorrect operator is typed. We might want to add an extra line directly after the OPERATOR? prompt that would read:

25 IF OP$ <> "+" AND OP$ <> "−" AND OP$ <> "*" AND OP$ <> "/" AND OP$ <> "C" THEN PRINT "INVALID OPERATOR" : GOTO 20

This will announce the error as soon as it is made and will give the user an immediate opportunity to correct it.

Another possible way in which an "idiot" might "crash" the program is by trying to divide by zero. Dividing a number by zero in BASIC is a major no-no, just as it is in general mathematics. Since dividing a number by zero is a meaningless operation, the computer will give an error message to anyone who tries to do it, thus interrupting the functioning of the program. Try it and see. Type / in response to the OPERATOR? prompt and 0 in response to a number prompt that follows. To avoid this error, we could change line 60 to IF OP$ = "/" AND N2 <> 0 THEN 300. This is yet another example of the sort of input error that a programmer must be very wary of.

Certainly this program is expandable. In fact, it could be the core of a much, much larger program. One way to expand the program would be to add new mathematical operations, in addition to those already included. For instance, many pocket calculators include a number of advanced mathematical functions such as sine, cosine, logarithm, square root, and raising a number to a power. (If you are not familiar with these terms, don't worry. They simply represent complex mathematical operations that have many uses in the sciences.) Since most versions of BASIC also include these operations, it would be simply a matter of expanding the section from lines 40 through 80 to incorporate a larger number of operators.

It might also be wise to add a way for the user to exit the program without pressing the BREAK key or turning off the computer. The letter "Q" (for Quit) is often used for this purpose, though "X" (for exit) is another possibility. It would be a simple matter to have the program end on input of such a symbol.

Finally, you might add a few more REM statements to the program, explaining to a prospective reader what various portions of the program do. They might even serve to freshen your own memory if you return to the program at a later date.

You might have some ideas of your own for other ways to expand this program. You are invited to rewrite it using the ideas expressed in this chapter, or to change it in ways of your own devising, adding new options or subtracting old ones, altering features until they are more to your liking, and making it work in a more efficient manner. When you are finished, you may even claim the program as your own. In a very real sense it will be, if you put a substantial amount of work into rewriting it. In the world of professional programming, many programs are the work of more than a single programmer.

There is no single, correct way to write a program, just as there is no one correct way to write a book or to sing a song, though there are many ways that are obviously wrong. Every programmer has his or her own style, just as writers and singers have their own styles. Obviously, you won't want to continue fiddling with a program forever, trying to make it better and better each time—especially if you write programs for a living. But there is a great deal of fun in playing with programs to see if they can be improved or simply be made to function in different, interesting ways. If you are a beginning programmer, this is a good way to learn to program.

This book is now at an end, but your "career" as a programmer has just begun. Use the techniques you learned in this book to construct programs of your own. Find new books on the subject of BASIC programming and learn advanced programming techniques. There is a great deal that we have not yet told you about this fascinating programming language. At some point, you may even want to go beyond BASIC and learn other programming languages.

There are also a great many computer magazines available at the larger newsstands. Some may be written specifically for the computer that you are using. These magazines often contain computer programs. If they are written for your computer, type them in and watch them work. Study them. See if you can understand how they do what they do. This is one of the better ways to learn how to write programs of your own.

And if you don't choose to continue studying computers, you at least have some understanding of how they work. In a world where computers are becoming increasingly common, you have stripped away a little of the mystery from these machines and prepared yourself for the long ride into the future.

You have learned a little magic and are ready to cast spells of your own. Your world will never again be quite the same.

Suggested Projects

1. Write a program of your own design and conception. If you don't have any idea right off of what kind of program you would like to write, the following projects offer some suggestions.

2. Write a simple game program. Most versions of BASIC offer a command for generating a random number within limits set by the programmer. (Usually this command is RND.) Check your manual to find out what that command is for your computer.

   Write a program for a game in which the computer thinks up a number (i.e., generates one at random) and you then try to guess what it is. If you guess too high, the computer will say TOO HIGH. If you guess too low, the computer will say TOO LOW. Have the computer count the number of guesses that you make. See how many guesses it takes to find a number between, say, 1 and 100.

3. Write a program that contains DATA statements of the names of several grocery items your family uses on a regular basis and the cost of each item. When you input the quantity of each item that is currently needed, it should print out the total cost of that item, and it should be capable of adding up the total cost of several different items, each at a given quantity.

4. Write a program, using the graphics capabilities that you discovered in your computer's manual after reading Chapter Eight, that will draw a small picture of a person on the video display and move that person about, as if he or she were walking back and forth across the screen.

A BASIC VOCABULARY

*(The words and symbols
of the BASIC language.)*

RESERVED WORDS

DATA. Precedes a list of data items to be read into variables with the READ statement.

FOR a = b TO c STEP d : (body of the loop) :NEXT. Creates a program loop from the word FOR to the word NEXT, which may be separated by as many program instructions (or program lines) as the programmer desires. The first time the loop executes, variable a will be assigned the value of expression b. On succeeding passes through the loop, the value of expression d will be added to the value of a, until the value of a exceeds the value of expression c, at which point the loop terminates and the computer begins executing the instructions following the word NEXT.

GOTO n. Transfers control to the program line numbered n.

IF a THEN b. If logical expression a is true, program statement b is executed.

INPUT a. Places a blinking cursor on the video display, accepts input from the keyboard, and stores that input at the memory location represented by variable a.

LET a = b. Assigns the value of expression b to variable a. The word LET is optional on most computers.

NEW. Clears the current program out of memory and prepares the computer to accept a new program.

NEXT. See FOR-TO-STEP:NEXT

PLOT a,b,c. Displays a pixel at coordinates a,b in color c.

PRINT a. Displays the value of expression a on the video display. Expression a may be string or numeric.

SET a,b,c. Used by some computers in place of PLOT a,b,c.

ARITHMETIC OPERATORS

+   addition
−   subtraction
*   multiplication
/   division

RELATIONAL OPERATORS

>   greater than
<   less than
<> not equal to
=   equal to
>= greater than or equal to
<= less than or equal to

LOGICAL OPERATORS

OR. Compares two expressions and indicates that they are true only if one or both is true.

AND. Compares two expressions and indicates that they are true only if both are true.

NOT. Changes the value of a logical expression from true to false or vice versa.

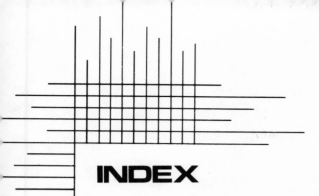

INDEX

ABOUT
THE
AUTHOR

Christopher Lampton is the author of more than twenty books of fiction and non-fiction, including several popular science First Books and Impact titles, as well as four science-fiction novels.

Chris became a computer enthusiast several years ago, when he acquired a Radio Shack microcomputer to use for word processing. Since then, he has learned a number of computer languages, become proficient in programming, and purchased four more computers. He is currently working on additional titles in the Computer Literacy series, as well as a microcomputer dictionary and a series of books on computer graphics, all for Franklin Watts.

Chris lives in Maryland, near Washington, D.C., and has a degree in broadcast communications.